MANAGEMENT
IN THE USA

uneuc.

MANAGEMENT IN THE USA

Peter Lawrence

SAGE Publications
London • Thousand Oaks • New Delhi

SAGE Publications Ltd
6 Bonhill Street
London EC2A 4PU

SAGE Publications Inc
2455 Teller Road
Thousand Oaks, California 91320

SAGE Publications India Pvt Ltd
32, M-Block Market
Greater Kailash – I
New Delhi 110 048

British Library Cataloguing in Publication data

A catalogue record for this book is available
from the British Library

ISBN 0 8039 7832 4
ISBN 0 8039 7833 2 (pbk)

Library of Congress catalog record available

Typeset by Mayhew Typesetting, Rhayader, Powys
Printed in Great Britain by Biddles Ltd, Guildford, Surrey

To Mike & Cynthia

Contents

Acknowledgements	viii
Preface	ix
1 Stars and Strands	1
2 An Economic Phenomenon	20
3 Individualism	37
4 Strategy	49
5 Proactivity	61
6 Systems	71
7 Free Speech and Self-interest	81
8 Industrial Relations	93
9 Personnel and People	102
10 Audit	115
11 An American Paradox	126
Bibliography	132
Index	135

Acknowledgements

I would like to thank the Owen Graduate School of Management at Vanderbilt University for their hospitality, support and facilitation. I had the benefit of two periods at Owen getting ideas from faculty, reading, and using Vanderbilt as a base for some of the fieldwork.

Central to the research that made the book possible is a large number of company visits and interviews with managers in various parts of the USA. I am most grateful to these companies and organisations for their openness and welcome, and to the individual managers for their time, indulgence, and friendly response. Furthermore, some of these managers also agreed to my request to spend a day or two with them as an observer of their everyday work. This was most generous spirited of them. I felt it added a lot to my understanding, and it was a lot of fun.

My Canadian friend Dwight Tanner has discussed with me a lot of the issues raised in the book, and also supplied me with a number of *bons mots* on American life and business which have found their way into the text.

I also had the opportunity to 'test run' a lot of the ideas on my friend Vince Edwards on our endless drives around America.

Three of my friends, Michael Johnson, Sara Keck and Sarah-Kay MacDonald, were kind enough to read part of the manuscript, and I am grateful to them for their comments and encouragement, and for the generous suggestion that I have understood at least something of the country of their birth.

Finally I would like to thank my secretary Ann Lewitt for preparing the manuscript.

Preface

In the early stages of writing this book it occurred to me that it was 15 years since I first 'unsheaved the pen' to write about management in a country other than my native Britain, and on that occasion it was West Germany. Since then I have done similar studies in a lot of countries, and written books about several of them, sometimes alone, sometimes with friends. After all this, it ought to be pretty easy; and that thought in turn provokes the question – was it?

Well some parts of the operation were quite easy; easier than an outsider might think. My inclination has always been to do these studies in a fairly hands on way, going to the country, living and working there for a while if that is possible, visiting lots of companies and interviewing a decent spread of managers. Well, considering how large America is, and how far away it is, all that turned out to be quite manageable: one just needs a bit of ingenuity. And a lot of this research activity can be set up in advance. One can fly to say Chicago for less than it costs to fly to Zürich, visit 10–12 companies by prior arrangement in five working days, and when you have done this sort of thing a couple of times you do not even experience jet lag on the flight east back home.

Human ageing also played a part. One of the effects of getting old, I find, is a tendency to get on and do it, just in case the chance doesn't come round again. And the same with financing the research: the trick seemed to be to get on with it, and worry about how to pay for it afterwards.

There is another way in which the undertaking was quite easy – sort of. This is that there was never any doubt that a characterisation of American management would be possible. A characterisation, that is, that assigned features to it, in broad brushstrokes, and differentiated it from management in other countries, at least in terms of degree. Before starting, it was clear that this would be possible, and some of the dimensions in terms of which it would be doable were also clear. This is not something that goes without saying; it is not always like this.

Again to speak personally, I recall going with a similar mission to Sweden in the early 1980s and being genuinely worried that the whole thing might be un-doable, that at the end of the day there would be nothing to say about Swedish management, nothing to differentiate it. Sure I had already looked at management in West Germany, as it then was, to good effect, and certainly there were points of contrast between Germany and Britain, but perhaps this was just a fluke, just a lucky break. Perhaps German management was uniquely interesting, perhaps Britain and Germany were polar types, or at least there were a limited number of different types (and Sweden would not be among them). Or, worst of all, Sweden would turn out to be a 'watered-down' version of Germany, and there would be no interesting tale to tell because the strong version of the tale had been told already.

Luckily this turned out not to be true, these fears were not justified. And in fact on all subsequent occasions sojourns in other countries (cultures) did throw up characterising possibilities, did yield contrasts, did provide 'tales to tell'.

Yet even with the benefit of hindsight, the USA is in a class of its own. That it will have a recognisable identity in matters of business and management is assured in advance. America is not one of these 'wishy-washy' countries about which no one can think of anything to say. It has a strong image in the wider world, is high profile, and everyone knows something about it. And such claims are even more true in matters of business and management. Business is the American priority, management is something they pretty well invented. In the post-war era American managers were everywhere, telling the rest of us how to do it! In this post-war period, indeed, there was much talk of 'the management gap', a phrase used to signal the shortcomings of the Europeans in running enterprises, a limitation that paralleled the technology gap, or the extent to which everyone else's technology fell behind that of the Americans.

Or again it seemed that there had always been American companies in Europe, and they proclaimed their Americanness. While lots of people in Britain may have thought that Philips was Welsh not Dutch, everybody knew that Ford and Heinz and Esso and Mars were American. Thousands of Europeans worked for American companies, had occasional trips to the USA, saw American executives 'come down among them', and more important than either of these became self-consciously enmeshed in American management systems.

But there is a downside to this, to all the familiarity and 'presence among us'. And this is that the familiarity structures our perceptions. Beginning research in the USA I could never replicate the magnificently empty mind I had taken to Sweden. This is not an exercise in false modesty. There is indeed something to be said for an empty mind, and this is that it gives reality a chance, that it is possible for reality to impose itself on individual consciousness precisely because of the absence of preconceptions and hypotheses up for testing.

To put it in a more down to earth way, it is much more difficult to say something original about America, and if I have risen to that challenge it will be only 'at the edges', in interpreting anew things that 'everyone knows', in positing relationships between cause and effect, in showing how various phenomena are consistent – with each other or with some determining value. For the most part I have merely formulated, put things into words; or elaborated, shown of what something consists, or shown how some phenomenon is variously manifested. And of course I have exemplified, I have illustrated and given examples – principally from interviews conducted with American managers in the early 1990s and from short periods spent as an observer in American companies.

Which brings us to the question, what is the substance, the 'evidence' on which this book is based? Well, it is a number of things, tiered:

- reading, and particularly the inferences one can make from books about management written by Americans (most of the world's stock, in fact)
- absorbing other people's impressions, listening to the views of (principally) European managers with American experience
- knowledge going back to the 1970s of American subsidiaries in Europe, particularly in Britain and Germany
- visiting a lot of companies in the USA and interviewing managers, particularly chief executives; doing this more or less systematically in three different areas – the North, the middle and the South
- doing a much smaller number of observational studies, where indulgent executives – in marketing or human resources management or general management – allowed me to trail them for a day or two, be a party to the action, sit in on the meetings, be a 'fly on the wall' (except that in proactive American culture it is rather more difficult to be merely a fly!).

Throughout I have been ready to give 'a warts and all' picture; not to conceal the conceit and the insularity, the sometimes heartless materialism, the lying and boasting, the breaking of laws and the foreshortening of reality. Yet this is no crudely negative portrait. There is much that is done well, there are innumerable interlocking strengths, there is energy, organisational drive. Yes, I am impressed, yes this is professional management.

At the same time the USA does not seem to be a rising economic power, in spite of the boom that began in the autumn of 1993. America seems to have lost the effortless superiority it enjoyed in business after the Second World War. Its great advantages seem somehow to have ebbed away. The rules of the game appear to have changed, and in changing have undermined American strengths and exposed weakness. America may still be the richest country, but the margin has been reduced, and the USA is no longer a mecca of unparalleled wealth.

Can these two facts – excellence in management and relative economic decline – be reconciled? Is the paradox resolvable? Certainly I have had a go at this problematic in the last chapter, but not comprehensively or decisively. At the end of the day I do not have any 'sure-fire' answers – but neither do 260 million Americans.

1

Stars and Strands

Americans are the damndest people!
Why can't everybody be like them?

Ernie Pyle

Ernie Pyle was a correspondent during the Second World War. The remark quoted above was inspired by his observing that some US Marines made pets out of baby goats on Okinawa. It points up three interesting facts about Americans.

First, they are interesting to themselves – have a consciousness of their difference, of being a bit special. Second, Americans are interesting to others: America is a most written-about society. All those who go there are inclined to record their views and impressions – from the French aristocrat to the British pop music journalist, from Anthony Trollope's mother to the founder of One-Upmanship. What other society has had this kind of attention, and for two hundred years? Third, American behaviour tends to be assertive, uninhibited, unselfconscious – at home and abroad. The message is: if you want to make a pet out of a baby goat – go for it.

Given these three facts it may well be asked, is there anything new to say? The answer is that there probably is if one changes the focus a bit. Rather than attempting to add to the dominant characterisation centring around equality–freedom–achievement–abundance it may be helpful to highlight a few angles that impinge on business and management, mostly in an indirect way. Let us start with the issue of national self-consciousness.

One way to get a feel for this national self-awareness is to visit America from Canada, preferably crossing the border by road. The transition is from an unassertive, mildly self-effacing country whose first value is order, to a more exuberantly nationalistic one whose first value is freedom. After crossing the line the accent is more twangy and distinctive; there are more flags, imperial eagles and nationalist emblems. Government buildings have flags, and so often do a range of non-official buildings from gas stations to holiday homes. The stars and stripes may be 'picked out' by plants and flowers in a public park, or in a private garden. Buildings carry a national legend – it is *US* mail, *state* high school, *federal* this and

American that. The advertising becomes more insistent and there is more of it – after all, the citizenry have a right to have their needs met, straight away and preferably with a choice of providers. Indeed one of the signs that the US border is close may be a sign telling you where you will find the first McDonald's – comforting to know this before leaving Canada. Distances, of course, are now measured in miles (no need for Canada's international gesture of using kilometres). The two countries are alike in their prodigal uses of space, yet there is greater immediacy, more uninhibited commitment to present purpose on the American side – it yields bigger concentrations, sharper images, a stronger sense of human will imposed on the world.

I would like to suggest that this American sense of self has its parallel in management. A distinctive feature of American managers is their ability to explain themselves. In a certain way they are perfect interviewees for the inquiring foreigner, very adept at making clear what they are doing, the means and ends of it, the way resources are being deployed, and how it all fits with a larger business system. They do not always realise that much of the reality they are describing for you is 'American flavoured'; indeed they are more inclined to assume that it is much about the same everywhere, but the awareness is still distinctive – knowing what they are at, where it leads, where it fits, how it relates to the big picture. This capability is not a universal feature among managers around the world. British managers, for example, are often shy of being so forcefully explicit; German managers are often too engrossed in functional and tangible specifics to map the system dynamics with American *élan*. Or again managers in Israel are typically too engrossed in the overly-exciting short-term issues to provide the ordered distance which is one ingredient of the American performance.

This phenomenon can be depicted in another way. This is to say that there is a consistency about American society. All its initiatives are driven by the same values, their effect is pervasive. And the style and practice of management is part of this consistency.

It might be helpful to make the point by means of a contrast with another country. Let us take France. It would be possible for a foreigner to visit France a lot as a tourist, and to get to know the country. One might develop a serious interest, perhaps learn French and then gain enhanced access to French culture and intellectual life. But all this would give the interested foreigner absolutely no idea of what it would be like to be a manager in a French company, of what strengths and weaknesses might be exhibited by French management in the round, of what the ethos of a French employing organisation would be like. And this is because there is compartmentalism in French life; it is because some French predilections are paradoxical – individualism and bureaucracy, for example, and because directness is not a French value.

But America is not France. America is a 'what you see is what you get' society. The nature of American management is exactly what you would infer from a general knowledge of the country, being marked by the same drives and presumptions.

This American management consciousness has another well recognised manifestation, and that is the behaviour of American companies abroad. The overseas corporate response is marked by assertion not adaptation. The expatriate US company does not seek to merge itself chameleon like in another culture. American companies abroad are recognisable, tend to be high profile, to proclaim their Americanness.

This is not a crude act of domination, but a set of behaviours based on corporate self-knowledge. The American understanding of the management task, the ability to articulate this understanding, and the self-confident executive interpretation all serve to render the American company abroad distinctive in the eyes of non-American beholders. And so does the plethora of planning and control systems that are the invariable accompaniment of the US subsidiary abroad.

Again this managerial self-awareness is reinforced by two other considerations. The first is easily expressed. It is clearly possible to distinguish between management as a concept, management as an activity, and management as a subject (Lawrence, 1986). Against the background of this distinction it could be fairly said that America invented management as a subject. The USA pioneered management education, established business schools nearly a century in advance of some of the other industrialised countries, and has made a disproportionate contribution to the management literature. Indeed most of the world's books on management have been written by people of American nationality. The USA also pioneered some of management's constituent subjects and specialities. So marketing for instance is an American invention, corporate strategy was developed first in the USA and most of the literature is American; or again scientific management started in the USA. Human relations is a largely American movement, American researchers/academics have contributed disproportionately to theories of motivation, understanding supervisory processes, and to studies of leadership and interaction.

The second factor that has served to reinforce American managerial self-awareness is historical. The USA emerged from the Second World War as *the* world economic power. In the appreciation of this economic pre-eminence two man-made considerations were conjoined with the natural advantages of size and resources, and these were American technology and American management.

With regard to the technology the emphasis was on means rather than ends, on know-how rather than on creativity. Americans would always be good at making things at lower cost, more efficiently, in large numbers, and at setting it all up so that quite ordinary people could do it on the basis of routine training. Systemisation was the leitmotiv.

But in this post-war epoch American management went beyond systems to become an ideology. The presumption was that American organisation was superior, their systems better integrated, their management more professional. It became common to speak of 'the management gap', the extent to which American management was superior to European management. The management gap was analogous to the technology gap: it conferred disadvantage on the Europeans but obligation as well as superiority on the Americans. Reducing the management gap became an American mission, a contribution to the post-war reconstruction of free Europe, less tangible than Marshall Aid but no less important.

This conviction was translated into a programme in the form of the Joint Productivity Councils, a vehicle that took thousands of British, French, German and other European managers across the Atlantic to gain at first hand an understanding of American methods (Locke, 1993). And when they had learned how to do it, they could go back to Europe and make it all happen, produce an economically viable Europe that could shoulder with America the burden of resisting communism.

Interestingly, both parties 'bought' the idea of the management gap. There was universal respect for American organisation and know-how, sometimes tempered (made bearable) by supercilious references to American shortcomings in history, culture and cuisine. The British, in particular, were strongly attracted by the American model: American resources were mouthwatering, American organisation was impressive, their apparent freedom from class consciousness was vicariously liberating, and to cap it all American companies preserved an enviable managerial prerogative against the assaults of organised labour.

The European recognition of American organisational superiority lasted at least into the 1970s. Consider, for example, the impact of Jean-Jacques Servan-Schreiber's famous book *Le Défi américain* (The American Challenge) that appeared in the late 1960s (Servan-Schreiber, 1967). The theme of the book was the American takeover of France by American multinationals. The book was a sensation, stayed on the bestseller lists for weeks. But consider why. Not just

French pride, or some simple anti-Americanism. The book struck a chord because the threat seemed real. An economic or at least a corporate takeover of France was credible. Because 'everyone knew' about American organisational superiority, those well-run companies with their know-how and methods and well-motivated managers would be next to irresistible.

America and Canada

There is another way into the problematic of American self-awareness and assertiveness. The relationship between America and Canada is gloriously asymmetrical. Americans seldom think about Canada. In their minds it is not significantly differentiated from the USA (it does not even have a separate country code for telephone dialling purposes – to call a Canadian number from the USA one just dials the Canadian city code as though it were an internal American call). Americans will regularly assert that Canadians are 'just like us'. There is an implicit assumption in the USA that economically Canada's future is tied to that of the USA, that some form of federation between the two states is inevitable. Americans sometimes refer with quiet pride to the fact that the 49th parallel, the border between the two states is the world's longest unguarded land frontier. But the key thing is that Canada is not important for Americans, it does not loom large in American consciousness, and all this is reflected in rather bland views.

The Canadians are made of sterner stuff. The relationship is important to them. Economically they are dependent on the USA (and hate it). Canada is a heavily export dependent country, and 70 per cent of their exports go to the USA. This dependency is underlined by three other factors. First Canada buys back from the USA things fashioned there from exported Canadian raw materials – processed fish and furniture for example. Second there is a further twist to the export dependency and this is that the various Canadian provinces have a penchant for trading with the *nearest* bit of the USA, which increases the immediacy and visibility of the dependence. So Canada's four Atlantic provinces, for example, export 70 per cent of their exports to the USA to the six American New England states. Third there is substantial one way cross-border shopping. Canadians within striking distance (liberally defined) will gladly shop at American malls, warehouses, supermarkets, and factory shops. The goods are cheaper, there is more choice, it is more fun and one can justify the whole affair by buying in bulk. What could be more fun for a Canadian family than a thousand-mile weekend drive down to Freeport, Maine to buy shirts by the dozen? Canadians are said to have the highest insurance spend per capita in the world (and are proud of this statistic, held to reflect Canadian caution and prudence): in part this reflects a need to insure against medical mishap on shopping visits to the USA!

But the phenomenon is not purely economic. For Canadians the USA is the 'significant other' country in a variety of respects, and they endlessly compare themselves with it and measure themselves against it. For Canadians a sense of national identity involves differentiating their country from the USA. One way in which they do this is to counterpose Canadian moderation to American excess. It goes like this:

Americans oversell, Canadians undersell
Americans move fast, Canadians move prudently
America tolerates extremes of wealth, Canada shows more social conscience
Americans are impatient of restraint, Canadians are mindful of the consequences of acts
American speech is direct and forceful, Canadian speech is restrained and conditional
and so on

Law and order comparisons naturally give Canadians much satisfaction, where they are able to claim that their crime rates are at West European levels (actually they are a bit higher, but let us not nitpick) and are nowhere near those of the USA, whose murder rate for example is four times higher than that of Canada. These differences again are reflected in the deportment of law and order enforcers, the police. Being a police officer is an eminently dangerous job in the gun-toting USA. Only taxi drivers and hotel desk clerks are more likely than police officers to be killed at work. But in Canada, the story goes, it is no big deal. Sure, Canadian police carry guns, but will not expect to use them. A Canadian policeman directing traffic will probably leave his gun belt in the patrol car: an American cop would not take off his gun even to have heart surgery.

The popular Canadian historian Pierre Berton has grouped and interpreted a lot of these differences by claiming that Canada is driven by a desire for order and America by a commitment to freedom (Berton, 1986). Berton illustrates this thesis very entertainingly, showing for example that the nineteenth-century gold rush towns of the Canadian Wild West, in contrast to their American counterparts, were citadels of Victorian prudery and regulated behaviour.

But American society put freedom first. The country was settled by people seeking freedom from. Freedom from oppression, from religious intolerance, from feudal obligations, and above all freedom from hunger and poverty. This starting emphasis on freedom *from* became a drive for freedom *to*. Freedom to compete, freedom to make the most of one's talents unrestricted by considerations of class or background, freedom to achieve, to succeed, to amass wealth, to amount to something, to distance oneself from one's origins and to take pleasure in socially acceptable boasting about it. And it is all underpinned by the Americans' inalienable right to 'the pursuit of happiness' actually written into the 1776 Declaration of Independence, which in practice has meant the right to do things that they hope will make them happy. And this in turn implies a high premium on safety, security and health; it implies wide consumer choice and a 'customer is king' ethos; it implies cheap and easy access for gratification and pleasurable experience (why else would America have more TV channels than any other country?). It also implies the right to keep trying until success and happiness are attained. So that in business a series of bankruptcies may be interpreted as representing a sustained drive for achievement which will surely work out in the end. The same phenomenon is observable in personal relationships, where there is a strong commitment to romantic love crossed with an unfettered choice of partner, high expectations invested in marriage, and frequent disappointment leading to the highest divorce rate in the world, topped off with a 'try again' mentality (re-marriage).

Freedom and business

This freedom ethic has underpinned the managerial assertiveness referred to earlier. It has implied a freedom from uncertainty, from hesitancy; it is an ingredient in American decisiveness in business. Foreigners who deal with Americans are often starkly aware of this decisiveness. Again the Canada contrast will point up the American essence. Canadians who deal in both countries, who are selling goods or services to organisations in both Canada and the USA, will tell you that in Canada you do not get to see the top person, that your proposed offering is filtered up the hierarchy and a decision eventually trickled down, and that when the decision is favourable it is still cautious – the organisation will try it out on a small scale, buy a hundred dollars' worth to see if they like it, work up to a big order. But in the USA you get to see the president, the decision is taken quickly, and if it is favourable they buy a million dollars' worth straight off. Something of this contrast is also seen in the banks of the two countries. Canadian banks exist to manage assets; they get it right by not getting it wrong. But American banks are there to cut deals and make profits, and every deal should be cut as quickly as possible so that one can get on to the next one.

The commitment to freedom naturally implies a desire to be free from constraint. Again this shows in the deportment of American companies as observed by non-Americans, where the tendency is to do it first and worry about any adverse consequences later; or to put it bluntly, American companies are more likely to be lawless if it suits them and to deploy resources such as lobbying, public relations effort and hired legal talent to get them out of any difficulties.

The same attachment to the idea of freedom from restraint is seen in the characteristically American espousal of the management prerogative, of management's right, that is, to act in its own corporate interests on its own judgement, without concession to other interests or consultation with other constituencies.

This distinctive American posture is nicely revealed in the attitude to industrial democracy, to some putative sharing of power with employees. Again it needs to be pointed up by an international comparison, but let us start at the beginning.

It is often asserted that management and workers have the same objectives. They are both, that is, committed to the success of the company; they both do well when the company does well. This formula is most convincing in times of boom and expansion. But when it comes to corporate behaviour in hard times, or even to the various means by which the end of corporate success is to be achieved, management and worker wishes often diverge.

Employees and their organised representatives will seldom accept workforce reductions, wage rate reductions, the scaling down of employee benefits, and certainly not rationalisation-driven plant closures or transfer of manufacturing facilities to low-wage areas beyond the national boundaries – even where a very strong case can be made for such moves in terms of the preservation of the company in a competitive environment. There are, of course, a few counter-examples from the early 1990s: North West Airlines, for instance, or the so-called Detroit 'give backs'.

Or if these issues seem too stark, consider that employees and their representatives tend to favour seniority-based promotion to, for example, supervisory positions, whereas management wants merit-based promotions. Workers like remuneration to be based on age and grade, management like it to be performance related. If lay-offs are inevitable workers think 'last in, first out' is a fair rule; management prefers 'worst guy, first out'! Or again, if there is a shortage of orders, management will be keen that jobs should be done quickly and completed orders delivered on time to customers, because good delivery performance is a competitive weapon. In the same situation workers will be inclined to make a meal of available work, spin it out to keep everyone occupied, because who knows where the next job is coming from?

In short, while both parties may want a successful company, they will frequently clash as to ways and means, priorities and principle. This divergence of interest has to be managed. Industrial democracy, sharing decision-making power with employees, is one way to manage it. Let us take as an exemplary case Sweden.

Since the Saltsjöbaden agreement of 1938 when employers and unions opted for peaceful co-existence Sweden has had, taking a middle-term view, stable and orderly industrial relations. This country has a strong trade union movement, and a union membership rate which is one of the highest in the world (and at least four times higher than the rate for the USA). Sweden established an industrial democracy system in the 1960s and topped it off with the 1976 Codetermination Act which gave the employee representative body at plant level, what is called the MBL Committee, the right to discuss anything with management, to institute negotiations on anything they like. While this Swedish system confers less in the way of tangible rights on the employee representative bodies than say the classic German co-determination system, the Swedish variation does indicate a more diffuse commitment to power sharing.

What are the consequences of Sweden's choice? For the most part stable, orderly and predictable relations between employers and employees. Good industrial relations in the formal sense of low strike rates/days lost by strike. Also rather good industrial relations at workplace level. While much may be questioned and discussed, there are for the most part few of the disruptions, refusals and work discipline violations that have been so much part of say British Industrial life (Lawrence, 1984).

But from a management viewpoint there is a price to pay. By definition industrial democracy restricts management's prerogative. The Swedish system means slower decision-making, albeit with faster implementation. There is also a repression of management initiative in the sense that the individual manager may not take initiatives he or she would view as desirable in the interests of efficiency or cost-reduction or whatever, for fear of employee resistance or because of reluctance to engage in all the hassle that 'selling' the initiative to workers' representatives would involve. The fact that this initiative repression is not observable and certainly not measurable does not make it any less real. And then again there is the commitment of management time to discussions with employee representatives – putting the case, defending the case, responding to employee requests for information, and so on.

If then the task is to manage the operational differences of interest between management and workers, and in the Swedish case it is achieved with co-determination, how have the Americans responded to this challenge? The answer can be simply expressed: the Americans have done exactly the opposite.

In the American case the management prerogative comes first, and is to be preserved at all costs. Management makes no pretence of wanting to work with trade unions, will seek to limit trade union power, and to drive hard bargains. For companies whose labour force is not unionised, preventing unionisation will be a constant war aim. There is, of course, no European-style co-determination, and there is no pressure to adopt or develop such a system. American executives, in fact, cannot usually be brought to a rational discussion of the pluses and minuses of worker democracy, so ingrained is their conviction that it cannot be right for management to limit its right to decide and to act as it sees fit (worker democracy indeed is commonly dismissed as 'communistic').

What the Americans gain in this way is:

- the psychological gains for executives that follow from the preservation of management prerogative
- fast decision-taking
- free decision-making in the sense that the whole range of options can be explored; none of them have to be screened-out 'for political reasons'
- no repression of initiative, as demonstrated in the case of Sweden
- the stance earlier described as an important condition of American decisiveness, a feature of management style in the USA that usually strikes foreign observers

There are losses, of course. Where management goes ahead and does what it wants without consultation, implementation may be more difficult, and take more time. Management action is more likely to generate resistance or antagonism. Employees cannot be appealed to in terms of reasonableness (a voluntary relinquishing of one-sided self-interest) or common values. Indeed employee compliance has to be bought with deals.

But our purpose here is not to say whether it is the Americans or the Swedes who have got it right, but to draw attention to the nature of the choice, and to underline the fact that the American choice is consistent and indicative.

Knowledge and information

It is possible to make a general distinction between information and knowledge, where information is best understood as simple facts, often in quantified form, whereas knowledge implies a context, meaning and understanding. Against the background of this distinction I would like to draw attention to the American passion for information.

There are three things that are remarkable about the information phenomenon in the USA:

Everyone likes information
It is readily available
This has implications for business

The popularity of information probably derives from the crossing of two values – achievement and egalitarianism. The possession of information may be a prerequisite for decision, will structure action, and facilitate control – and all these are part of achievement, which is widely desired in American culture. So information is central, can be pithily expressed and rapidly absorbed, is a convenient commodity for a busy and active people. And unlike knowledge, there is nothing elitist or exclusive about information. It does not require preparation or reflection, nor is a high educational threshold needed. Information is both a leveller and a minor contribution to social cohesion. Americans exchange information in the social space that the British fill by talking about the weather.

Indeed there is a tendency for information to drive out knowledge. Or at least to redefine knowledge, in the sense of thinking that if you had *more* information you would have the complete picture, that would be it, and there would not be anything else you would need to know or understand.

Or to put it another way, in any discussion or in the exploration of any issue Americans come more quickly to the point of wanting/ needing information. Consider as a homey example a simple newspaper story about the development of two adjacent communities – Richland Hills and North Richland Hills – in the Dallas–Fort Worth area of Texas. The essence of the story is how the development of these two communities diverged, with the Cinderella town of North Richland Hills, founded later and without the advantage of being on the Forth Worth loop (ring road), overtaking its elder sister. The 'fact box' (Figure 1.1) makes it all clear:

These figures – mean family income, median home value, tax rate – are food and drink to Americans. What in Europe would be handled qualitatively or in terms of 'more or less' propositions along the lines of 'residential property will tend to be more expensive in North Richland Hills', in America will be made explicit and quantified.

The information that Americans collect, collate and dispense is truly amazing – for its ingenuity, range and sometimes its downright

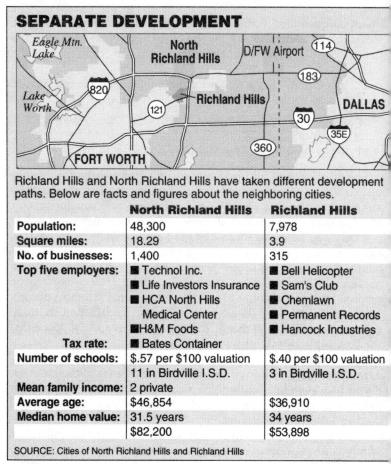

Figure 1.1

Source: *Dallas Morning News*, 29 March 1994. Reprinted with permission.

zaniness. For a quick introduction readers are invited to dip into the 1980-founded American paper *USA Today*, which offers daily colour-coded fact boxes on the socio-economic interstices of American life. Would you like to know the top towns for murder per head of population for 1993? No problem:

Gary, Indiana
Memphis, Tennessee
Washington, DC

Or top states for SAT (scholastic aptitude tests) scores?

Iowa
North Dakota
South Dakota
Utah
Minnesota
(Look for the pattern)

From the same source one could learn the breakdown of amateur versus professional fire brigades, broken down by rural versus urban location; cheapest and most expensive states for car insurance; the increase in sales of rubber gloves since the onset of Aids; and even the likelihood that your marriage partner is sleeping around, by size of community.

A German commentator on America once observed that their directness and investigative leanings made them bad diplomats but good journalists (Kronzucker, 1989) and the same blend of ingenuity and persistence can be seen in the unearthing and contriving of facts. The whole operation also confirms the suggestion made at the outset that America is a self-aware, self-interested society. The best American facts are facts about America. Information is richest when it deals with American lifestyle, behaviours, and above all consumer patterns. Consider for example the fun Americans have had from their postal codes.

Zip codes (ZIP stands for Zone Improvement Plan) were introduced in 1962 by the US Postal Service and eventually the country came to be divided into 36,000 zips. In the 1970s Jonathan Robbin, a computer scientist, had the idea of matching Zip codes with census data and consumer surveys to yield 40 lifestyle clusters. Robbin set up a marketing consultancy company to advise corporate clients on how to tailor their products and sales pitches to these various lifestyle clusters. Robbin proudly declared: 'Tell me someone's zip code and I can predict what they eat, drink, drive, even think.'

The whole enterprise was popularised by a subsequent book, *The Clustering of America*, by Michael Weiss, extending the concept and documenting the 40 clusters in some detail (Weiss, 1988). Needless to say the 40 clusters have been given labels both zappy and evocative, for instance:

Furs & Station Wagons: new money in metropolitan bedroom suburbs
Shotguns and Pickups: crossroads villages serving the nation's timber and bread-basket needs

| Single City Blues | downscale (= downmarket) urban, singles district |

These innocent zip codes prove to have a lot of sociometric mileage. Robbins/Weiss can tell us, for example, what are the top five and bottom five clusters for eating at McDonald's; or for joining the US army; or for shopping at K-Mart. They can even distinguish between top Coca-Cola consumers and top Pepsi consumers (except that the same cluster is top of both lists, called *Hard Scrabble*) this cluster of zip codes being made up of the nation's poorest, rural settlements.

Just to give a better idea of the substance of these cluster variations we will compare two of the clusters with regard to lifestyle: to make it more discriminating we will avoid an obvious cross-class contrast or a rural versus urban one and take instead two rural clusters, *Grain Belt* and *Back-Country Folk*.

Grain Belt of course is the rural Midwest, with a lot of zips from Iowa, Minnesota, Nebraska and Kansas. *Back-Country Folk* are in backwater rural areas, mostly in the old South (especially the Appalachians) and bits of the south-west such as the Ozark mountains in Arkansas and the Texas Panhandle. Weiss offers *high usage* (= preference) and *low usage* (= rejection) lists for TV programmes, food, cars, and newspapers and magazines, but probably the most accessible parts of the contrast for non-American readers will be the miscellaneous *Lifestyle* lists. The *high usage* contrast gives us:

Grain Belt	*Back-Country Folk*
Gas chain saws	Compact pick-ups
Cats	Canning jars and lids
Watch rodeo	Chewing tobacco
Canning jars	TV mail-orders
Tupperware	Wood-burning stoves
Horseback riding	Personal loans
Pianos	Civic clubs
Fresh-water fishing	Hunting
	Gospel records/tapes

While *low usage* yields:

Grain Belt	*Back-Country Folk*
Stamp collecting	Comedy records/tapes
Health clubs	Travel agents
Jazz records/tapes	Live theatre
24-hour teller cards	Imported champagne
Travel by cruise ship	Money-market funds

Sailing	Health clubs
Common stock	Downhill skiing
Burglar alarm systems	Environmental organisations

Differences that are fascinating to a rich, consumerist society; and especially so for a society whose business establishment invented marketing.

The information capability we have outlined and illustrated in the last few pages relates to business and management in a number of ways. Most obviously it both expresses and facilitates the practice of marketing and its associated promotional initiatives. Not only did Americans invent marketing as a subject, they also produced most of the world's marketing literature. And all the marketing gurus – Kotler, Levitt, and so on – are of course American. Even more important is the priority given to marketing in American companies, and the rigour and energy with which marketing practice is invested. Marketing is invariably a high-status function/department in American companies and for companies in FMCG (fast moving consumer goods) industries it is *the* function.

There is a further twist to the information–marketing relationship. Ever since Lord Leverhulme said, 'Half my advertising is wasted, but I don't know which half', there has been a struggle to 'make the connection'. Whether it is about 'mail-shotting', telephone cold-calling, or publication-based advertising there is an ever-growing desire to *target* potential customers, which will help to make a fortune for the likes of Jonathan Robbin, king of the zip codes.

There are two other considerations, rather less obvious. The first is to say that one feature of American management is the centrality of control systems. There are always objectives, there is always a plan, buttressed by a control system whose function is to show whether the objectives are being achieved. And the point is that control systems are information driven. One always needs to know things like: what are our costs, how many did we sell, how much profit are we making in Kansas, and so on. And if you don't 'make your numbers', you'd better have a good reason, or an up-to-date CV!

The second and overlapping point is that information structures decisions. This is a universal truth, but one that has particular application in the USA. This is so because American companies have a penchant for programmatic decisions. This is where it is 'clearly understood' that when X arises you do Y. When sales revenue in a given foreign country reaches a certain level you establish a manufacturing facility there to service that market; when the cost of overtime working in the factory reaches 25 per cent of all labour costs, shift work is implemented; where current orders are 20 per cent above normal manufacturing capacity some work is subcontracted; when revenue for a branch of the bank falls below a certain level the branch is closed – and so on. These are paratypical American decisions, where the decision in principle has already been taken (= is built into the rule) and 'the decision is taken' when the decision point is reached. And how do you know when the decision point has been reached? Easy: you collect and collate information, and the accretion of information will trigger the decision.

In these last two points – information for control, and information to structure decisions – it is not pretended that it is *the same* information as is to be found on the colour-coded fact boxes of *USA Today*. The point is rather that a society that likes information, that shows ingenuity and resource in gathering information, that runs on information, will find it natural to support management's informational needs, to make this a strength of American management.

Means and ends

Because of the optimism Americans brought to their country, the resources they found, and the talent for organisation they developed, Americans became inclined to the belief that anything is possible. People can shape their destiny. If you will it, it will be possible: it is only a matter of resource allocation, planning and organisation.

Indeed in the mid-twentieth-century golden age America seemed to have amazing achievements to its credit. That America was different from other countries, capable of responses and initiatives on a grander scale, first became obvious in the Great Depression of the 1930s, which itself was on a grander scale than the Depression in Europe. The Depression in the USA brought Roosevelt and the Democrats to power, with their New Deal programme, the essence of which was that government would initiate, innovate, proact and at the end of the day spend its way out of the Depression. As David Potter suggests in his interpretation of the American people *People of Plenty*, the whole programme was based on Roosevelt's conviction that America with its vast resources could not be poor, could not fail, could not fail to recover from the travails of the early 1930s (Potter, 1954). All one had to do was change the rules for a bit, spend, make work, establish public work schemes, dam the Tennessee river, start a welfare boom, improve the infrastructure and plan for prosperity. What else could Roosevelt have meant when he observed at the start of his March 1933 inauguration speech:

The only thing we have to fear is fear itself!

Roosevelt's choice to head the newly established Federal Relief Agency, Harry Hopkins, distinguished himself by spending $9 million in his first hour in office: his first act was to send telegrams to the governors of the (mostly Southern) poorest states asking them how much they needed and then authorising them to draw funds against federal guarantees.

The rest of the twentieth century was to offer further evidences of American capability. America acted as the arsenal of democracy, and more, in the Second World War. The USA largely paid for the Allied victory over the Axis Powers. Soon after the war the Americans paid to save the defeated Germans from starvation (Lawrence, 1980), and then they paid for the reconstruction of Western Europe with Marshall Aid, or more properly the European Recovery Programme. America acted as the bulwark against world communism, guarded the West, and cranked up the world economy after every recession. They developed the Salk vaccine and saved much of the world from the scourge of polio. They saw to 'little things' like the elimination of malaria on the island of Sardinia. They put a man on the moon. They outspent and technologically outflanked the former USSR with 'Star Wars' and helped to bring an end to European communism. This is some record.

There are parallels to all this in American business:

- there is a belief in initiatives, in conscious, explicit intentions to move to change
- there is a corresponding belief in programmes, in planned and coordinated sets of actions to achieve objectives; in the context of the mid-1990s, for example, just about every American corporation embraced TQM (total quality management)
- their scale advantages and innate optimism means that American companies tend to respond to challenges positively, and to seek to solve them with organisation and resources (rather than with ingenuity); Americans have not had much experience in figuring out how to do it with $10

To take the last idea, and push it down to the level of manager behaviour, American managers confronting problems, acting singly or in groups, tend to move quickly to solutions. The analysis is only a means to the end (solution) and not invested with any *sui generis* interest. Indeed if the analysis is not in quantitative or financial form it may well be a bit slighted. And when it comes to solutions the kind that are preferred are ones that are tried and tested, that have worked 'someplace else'. There is not a requirement that the solution should be marked by elegance (as in France) or technical virtuosity (as in Germany) or by ingenuity (as in Britain).

There is another twist to this saga of means and ends. Because Americans start from the premise that everything is possible, it follows that every end must have means. But more cynical Europeans think they know that not everything is possible, and therefore there are some ends for which appropriate means are lacking. But, to continue the European view, Americans don't know this, so when there are desirable ends they will go ahead with inappropriate means.

A very worthwhile book by Robert Levering and Milton Moskowitz, *The 100 Best Companies to Work for in America*, which gives pen-portraits of the chosen companies with lots of employee testimony, offers a few examples of this phenomenon (Levering and Moskowitz, 1993). Consider for instance the initiatives of the president of Algasco, Alabama's largest distributor of natural gas, one Mike Warren, newly appointed in 1984. Warren is keen to promote management–employee solidarity. He wants to take the company up to the heights and to take the workforce with him:

> Warren first met all 1,300 employees to tell them his vision. In the spring of 1985 he visited all the company's service areas and met with groups of from a dozen up to as many as 50 employees. According to Warren: 'It was the first time they had that kind of meeting with the president of the company'. Often he began by serving the employees cheeseburgers that he grilled on a barbeque he carted around on the back of his car. At one location Warren took half an hour out of his schedule to play basketball with crewmen and servicemen on the company basketball court.

Two simple questions. Can you imagine a European doing this? And if not, why not? Try another example. This time it is Ben & Jerry's Homemade, a premium ice-cream company in Vermont. It prides itself on being a no status, no nonsense, fun place to work in. Levering and Moskowitz give it five stars for camaraderie and friendliness.

> Executives hold quarterly meetings to keep employees up to date. These sessions are far from run of the mill presentations. In the past they have had midnight meetings to accommodate the third shift, where everyone else arrives dressed in pyjamas. When communication was chosen as the theme of one employee meeting, every employee received a set of wax lips. At some meetings they turn on the strobe light and dance to rock and roll music after business is done.

One might reformulate the idea and say that American convictions as to the efficacy of means seem to work for them. While Europeans may be unconvinced and look askance at American 'excesses', it is important for those same Europeans to recognise the model to which the Americans are working.

I have tried in this first chapter to throw up a few ideas about America's past and the nature of its society, and to relate them to business practice in a general way. In subsequent chapters the focus will be more particular – on various aspects of management and manager behaviour.

2

An Economic Phenomenon

This is a book about management, not economics, but a little economic scene-setting may still be helpful. So I will offer some brief observations on the history, substance, and apparent destiny of the American economy.

History

Historical reviews of the genesis of the modern American economy tend to highlight three considerations. The first of these concerns the plenitude of (economic) national advantage conferred on the area that became the USA. The size of the country, the range of natural resources, the land that could be brought into cultivation, the range of things that could be grown, the natural harbours and navigable rivers. This has, of course, all been said before, it is true and relevant, but there is something else that should be added to this testimony. This is that raw material and natural resource endowment alone do not make for a mighty economy. Both Australia and Canada are richly endowed in the same way as America; and while both have produced a high standard of living for their citizens based on natural resource exploitation, they have not done very much else. What distinguished the USA is that in addition to these natural resource advantages the country developed manufacturing industry on a grand scale. At its simplest it is this combination of resources and industry that made the USA an economic superpower.

The second point that is often urged is that the shortage of manpower in America as it was developing economically in the nineteenth century put a premium on the development of 'labour saving' machinery in production. Now this is not a proposition that lends itself to scientific testing, but common sense and a review of the inventions that occurred suggest that this consideration is true and relevant as well.

Thirdly it is commonly asserted that the construction of the American railroads in the 19th century led to an early familiarity with and acceptance of joint stock financing. The argument goes like this. Because of the size of the country, and the at times precarious nature of political unity, the railways were more important to the

USA than to most other countries, and necessarily on a larger scale (none of the 11 miles from Stockton to Darlington that made history in Britain). The scale of the financing was commensurate with the geographic scale of construction, and as such well beyond the means of any individual entrepreneur, however substantial his or her personal wealth. In consequence the railroads could only be financed and built by selling shares. Notwithstanding the corruption and cupidity that this operation gave rise to, in London as well as in the USA, it is held, no doubt with good sense, that the early exposure to joint stock financing was a necessary condition for the early emergence of manufacturing companies that were large by European standards.

To this listing of sensible and conventional ideas I would like to add two more. The first of these is about the origin of management. In the introductory chapter it was suggested that in talking about management one can usefully distinguish between management as a concept, management as an activity, and management as a subject. In the previous chapter we argued that it was the USA that developed management as a subject, and both pioneered and power housed its teaching. It is also quite reasonable to argue that it was America that developed the concept of management. There is a difference, that is, between the activity, what managers do, and the consciousness of that activity, what we are calling here the concept of management. This same shortage of people in the developing USA that is held to put a premium on mechanical aids and labour-saving inventions, when crossed with the infinite opportunities offered by newly settled territory, also puts a premium on entrepreneurship, versatility, and the effective use of limited resources, namely managing! I would like to suggest that there are reasons inherent in the dynamics of nineteenth-century American society that led the USA rather than any other country to develop a consciousness of management as something that can be extrapolated from discrete tasks and be made the subject of analysis, generalisation and exhortation. And while this American predisposition to take out the management and talk about it has influenced thinking and practice in many other countries, it is not the only way in which management can be understood. In some of the European countries, that is, the tendency would be to regard management as a part of many jobs and callings, not all of them 'managerial'. It is this isolation and identification of management as the key variable that seems to me to be the legacy of nineteenth-century America.

The next issue is something that is observable rather than explainable. Somehow or other America in the 19th century seemed to generate a business dynamic, to confront its citizens with business exigences, these having more salience than in European countries. Take for example the American farmer.

In the colonial period at least there seem to have been sturdy, independent, self-sufficient, largely subsistence farmers depending on local milling, tanning and milking services (Cochran and Miller, 1942) – an American genre immortalised out of all proportion in popular myth. In practice these farmers do not seem to have lasted very long. Competition from the cities closed down local services, and the new providers had to be paid in cash rather than produce. At the same time the farmers and their families became increasingly dependent upon factory-made goods that had to be paid for too. End of subsistence farming, switch to cash crops. Enter problems of capitalisation, market intelligence and yield calculation.

For these eastern farmers or their descendants who moved on (west) the involvement in business considerations was intensified by the simple fact that they had to buy the land from someone, and then had to budget for cash flow and loan repayments. The development of major agricultural machinery in mid-century added a further complication: if a farmer did not buy a reaper binder his farm was less productive than his neighbour's; if he did buy one, more debts and more repayment calculations ensued.

After the Civil War the prairies and great plains were settled, and the business ethos intensified again. Mortgaged farmers were now far removed from centres of population, and were heavily dependent upon the East Coast providers of finance and rail freight services. The most important determinant of their professional success was nothing to do with cultivation or animal husbandry. It was price.

This ever-present all encroaching climate of business that I have sought to illustrate with the example of the American farmer probably has both a positive and a negative genesis. On the one hand it is the product of this newness, size and scale of the country; on the other side there are none of the traditions or institutions of old Europe to impede the march of business.

Substance

Wisse Dekker, the former chief executive of the Dutch multinational Philips once told a story about an encounter with a Japanese businessman who had summed up his world view with the aphorism:

> America could produce all the world's food.
> Japan could produce all the world's manufactured goods.
> And Europe could become a discotheque.

Not only is this judgement a bit hard on Europe, it obscures the fact that America has been well placed to fill all three roles. In short America is big, and multi-capable.

Not only is the USA the world's largest economy, it is also the world's third largest country by area after Russia and Canada. Furthermore it is the world's third largest country by population after China and India. And according to the *US Statistical Abstract*, *New York City* (or probably the metropolitan area of New York) is the world's third largest town after Mexico City and Tokyo-Yokohama.

Natural resources

The USA is well represented in the world production of major mineral commodities, as Table 2.1 makes clear.

Table 2.1

	Leading producers 1992 (in order)
Mineral fuels	
Coal	China, *USA*, Russia
Dry natural gas	Russia, *USA*, Canada
Natural gas plant liquids	*USA*, Saudi-Arabia, Canada
Petroleum, crude	Saudi-Arabia, Russia, *USA*
Petroleum, refined	*USA*, Russia, Japan (for 1991)
Non-metallic minerals	
Cement, hydraulic	China, Japan, *USA*
Diamond, gem and industrial	Australia, Russia, Botswana,
Nitrogen in ammonia	China, *USA*, Russia
Phosphate rock	*USA*, China, Morocco
Potash, marketable	Canada, Belarus, Russia
Salt	*USA,* China, Germany
Sulphur, elemental basis	*USA*, Russia, China
Metals	
Aluminium	*USA*, Russia, Canada
Bauxite	Australia, Guinea, Jamaica
Chronite	Kazakhstan, South Africa, India
Copper	Chile, *USA*, Japan
Gold	South Africa, *USA*, Australia
Iron ore	China, Brazil, Australia
Lead	Australia, *USA*, China
Manganese	Ukraine, China, South Africa
Nickel	Russia, Canada, New Caledonia
Steel, crude	Japan, *USA*, China
Tin	China, Brazil, Indonesia
Zinc	Canada, Australia, China

Source: adapted from US Bureau of Mines, *Mineral Commodity Summaries*, 1994

Furthermore the USA is a major producer of wheat, at 66.92 million metric tons as of 1992, with only China, India and the former Soviet Union being ahead in absolute volume terms. With corn production of 140.774 million metric tons for the same year the USA is the world leader, with China in second place. In fish every country is a long way behind the world leader, Canada, but the USA is still in sixth place after Canada, Japan, Chile, the former Soviet Union and Peru, with a commercial catch of 5.473 million metric tons as of 1991. When it comes to meat production the USA is the world leader with 31,350,000 metric tons (carcass weight) for 1993; the former Soviet Union is in second place with about half this amount.

Manufacturing

American manufacturing output is, of course, enormous, as Table 2.2 shows (see pp. 25–7).

The two points to note are quite simply the range, the variety of industrial categories in which the USA has a presence, and the predominance of durable over non-durable goods. A variation on this is also apparent in the pattern of exports, that is to say, they show considerable diversity. The second point is about the substance of these exports.

Trade patterns

As of 1993 the top six countries as sources of American imports were:

$m	
Canada	110,922
Japan	107,288
Germany	28,605
UK	21,736
France	15,244
Italy	13,223

and the corresponding top six countries as recipients of American exports were:

$m	
Canada	100,147
Japan	47,949
UK	26,376
Germany	18,957
France	13,267
Netherlands	12,839

Table 2.2

Item	1980	1985	1986	1987	1988	1989	1990	1991
Current dollars (billions)								
Gross domestic product	2,708	4,039	4,269	4,540	4,900	5,251	5,546	5,723
Manufacturing	588	798	829	878	961	1,005	1,025	1,026
Durable goods	349	472	480	502	541	563	564	551
Lumber and wood products	19	24	27	31	32	33	31	30
Furniture and fixtures	8	14	14	15	16	16	16	16
Stone, clay, and glass products	18	24	26	24	24	25	25	23
Primary metal industries	44	36	37	36	43	46	44	42
Fabricated metal products	45	57	58	59	63	67	67	65
Machinery, exc. electrical	77	87	80	(X)	(X)	(X)	(X)	(X)
Industrial machinery and equipment	(X)	(X)	(X)	88	100	106	109	102
Electric and electronic equipment	55	84	85	(X)	(X)	(X)	(X)	(X)
Electronic and other electric equipment	(X)	(X)	(X)	77	81	87	86	88
Motor vehicles and equipment	27	58	58	59	59	53	46	41
Other transportation equipment	26	48	54	57	56	60	65	65
Instruments and related products	20	27	28	40	50	52	56	59
Misc. manufacturing industries	10	14	14	15	17	18	19	19
Non-durable goods	239	327	349	376	420	442	461	475
Food and kindred products	52	72	74	79	83	88	97	102
Tobacco manufactures	7	11	13	13	14	14	16	17
Textile mill products	15	17	19	20	20	21	22	22
Apparel and other textile products	17	21	22	23	24	25	25	26

continued overleaf

Table 2.2 *(continued)*

Item	1980	1985	1986	1987	1988	1989	1990	1991
Paper and allied products	23	33	35	39	44	47	46	45
Printing and publishing	33	52	57	61	65	71	72	73
Chemicals and allied products	48	67	73	82	94	100	104	106
Petroleum and coal products	24	24	26	26	41	38	40	43
Rubber and misc. plastics products	17	26	27	30	31	34	35	36
Leather and leather products	4	4	3	3	4	4	4	4
Constant (1987) dollars								
Gross domestic product	3,776	4,280	4,405	4,504	4,719	4,838	4,897	4,861
Manufacturing	725	811	819	878	924	932	929	908
Durable goods	424	468	472	502	536	543	537	526
Lumber and wood products	22	25	28	31	30	29	28	26
Furniture and fixtures	12	14	14	15	15	15	14	14
Stone, clay, and glass products	24	25	26	24	25	26	26	23
Primary metal industries	49	35	39	36	34	33	35	37
Fabricated metal products	55	58	56	59	62	61	60	57
Machinery, exc. electrical	81	78	75	(X)	(X)	(X)	(X)	(X)
Industrial machinery and equipment	(X)	(X)	(X)	88	97	102	102	101
Electric and electronic equipment	70	83	84	(X)	(X)	(X)	(X)	(X)
Electronic and other electric equipment	(X)	(X)	(X)	77	85	91	91	94
Motor vehicles and equipment	40	63	58	59	63	57	49	41
Other transportation equipment	38	47	51	57	58	61	64	61
Instruments and related products	24	27	27	40	50	50	50	54
Misc. manufacturing industries	10	14	14	15	17	17	17	17

Non-durable goods	301	342	348	376	387	389	392	383
Food and kindred products	64	75	73	79	82	79	84	84
Tobacco manufactures	20	14	15	13	12	10	9	8
Textile mill products	17	18	19	20	20	21	21	21
Apparel and other textile products	20	21	22	23	24	25	24	24
Paper and allied products	31	36	37	39	40	39	42	42
Printing and publishing	53	59	59	61	63	64	62	58
Chemicals and allied products	58	67	75	82	83	84	88	86
Petroleum and coal products	15	23	19	26	30	31	26	23
Rubber and misc. plastic products	19	26	26	30	30	32	32	32
Leather and leather products	5	4	3	4	4	4	4	4

X Not applicable.

Source: US Bureau of Economic Analysis, *Survey of Current Americans*, May and November 1993

Of the seven countries that figure in the two lists the USA has a favourable balance of trade only with the UK and the Netherlands. The biggest single trade deficit is as one might expect, with Japan, where the USA imports more than twice as much as it exports.

The same source, the 1994 *Barclays Bank Country Report* for the USA notes the greater importance of consumer goods in imports and of capital goods in exports. To offer an alternative perspective, however, Michael Porter (1990) draws attention to a trend in American exports. Reviewing the top 50 American industries in terms of world export share as of 1985 he notes:

> For many Americans accustomed to thinking of the United States as an advanced industrial nation, this list may come as a surprise. Of the top twenty-five industries, fifteen are heavily based on natural resources (as are twenty-two of the top fifty) (Porter, 1990b: 508)

In other words, in terms of the content of its exports the USA appears to be becoming more like Canada and Australia, and less like Germany and Japan. Perhaps Wisse Dekker's Japanese interlocutor was on to something after all.

Sectors and services

Economists distinguish between the primary, secondary and tertiary sectors of the economy. Primary is agriculture, fishing and extractive industries; secondary is manufacturing; and tertiary is services. It is the last of these, the tertiary sector, which tends to cause problems of interpretation since this tertiary sector is quite heterogeneous, including everything from bartenders to brain surgeons, sales clerks to research scientists.

A trend during the last 40 years of the twentieth century has been a progressive shift from the secondary to the tertiary sectors in the advanced industrial countries, typically eventuating in a situation where more people are employed in the tertiary than in the secondary sector. Among the major industrial countries the first to reach this stage where tertiary preponderates over secondary was the USA. At the time (1960s and 1970s) this was viewed positively, as a mark of modernity. The term post-industrial society was coined for this development, and the implication was that post-industrial was a whole lot nicer (cleaner and cooler) than industrial. Now the feeling is that it is more difficult to interpret the phenomenon.

Table 2.3 shows the position of America in comparison with other advanced countries.

Table 2.3 *International comparison of structure of employment (1992)*

Country	Composition (%)		
	Primary	Secondary	Tertiary
USA	2.9	24.2	72.9
UK	2.1	27.6	70.3
France	5.7	28.2	66.1
Japan	6.4	34.1	59.5
Italy	8.8	31.9	59.3
Germany	3.6	39.0	57.4

Source: adapted from *Japan 1994: An International Comparison*, Book of Japan, Tokyo, 1995

These figures are interesting in the similarity they posit between the USA and UK, and even more in the contrast between the USA and Japan and still more between the USA and Germany (Germany was the last of the advanced countries to 'cross the line' from manufacturing to services). But if we focus on the internal American relativities, what do the figures tell us?

The answer is probably that they tell us several different things, and it will be difficult to disaggregate these. First, these figures are proportions, so as one goes down another goes up. And we know that thousands of jobs are lost in manufacturing each year (figures are given in the last chapter) so the high figure for the tertiary sector in part reflects a decline in industrial employment. Second, as suggested above, post-industrial society euphoria is a thing of the past; a lot of the jobs in America's tertiary sector are low-wage ones – in fact the fastest growing occupational category in the USA is that of retail clerk/sales assistant. But this is not the whole story.

International transactions and the service sector

For most of the 1980s and for the 1990s so far, the USA has seen a current account deficit, that is, the value of imports has exceeded that of exports. Indeed the *Barclays Bank Country Report* cited earlier gives a deficit of $97 billion for 1993 on the balance of trade in goods. But if we turn to services there was a surplus for the same year of $43 billion. In other words, the burgeoning service sector in the USA is not to be interpreted solely in a residual way or in terms of displacement from manufacture. The USA has strengths in services.

Consider, for example, credit cards. Here the USA has a virtual monopoly. Or car rental. This activity was pioneered by the USA, American car rental companies enjoy market dominance, and nearly all the international players are American. International hotel chains are another American strength, including Hilton, Hyatt, Marriott, Sheraton, Best Western, and originally Holiday Inn. Similarly the USA has international fast food chains including Pizza Hut, Kentucky Fried Chicken, Pizzaland, the ubiquitous McDonald's, and, more selectively the Chicago Pizza Pie Factory, Hard Rock Cafe, and Planet Hollywood. Air transportation is another example. Most countries have at the most one megacarrier, with a number of the European national airlines faltering in the mid-1990s. Now the USA has at least two megacarriers, notwithstanding the demise of Pan American in 1991 and the problems experienced by TWA.

In retailing it is accepted wisdom that taking national chains into other countries is a precarious operation. In Europe the relatively small number of success stories – Ikea of Sweden, Body Shop and Laura Ashley in Britain and above all Benetton of Italy – are universally lauded. And indeed it might be thought that Europe, whose key characteristic is heterogeneity and whose presumptive strength is the management of diversity, has an advantage here. But the USA also has achievements in cross-border retailing, with Gap in youth fashion, specialist trainer-sportswear shops such as Foothold and Footlocker, and, originally, Safeway in grocery. And moving from retail to fashion, again the USA has international achievements. Not only in jeans – Levis, Wrangler, Lee – but also in broader range of fashion goods such as Ralph Lauren, Karl Lagerfeld and Calvin Klein.

Interestingly, there is a link between some of these successes in service industry and recent social history. A number of these successes, that is to say, relate to international travel – the credit cards, hotel chains, car rentals and air transport. This ensemble dates from a post-Second World War period when only Americans travelled abroad in numbers sufficient to affect the type and level of service provided for the expatriate masses!

There is another issue. In Chapter 6 I document and explore the American penchant for systems, with primary reference to manufacturing industry. Yet this flair for systems is very relevant to service provision. This American aptitude for specification – standardisation – quality assurance – operational control is immensely important in enterprises such as hotels and fast food. This is clearly an area where American businesses enjoy competitive advantage.

The age of self-doubt

In the 1970s America presented a worrying picture to the outside world. This world had grown accustomed to American might, resolution and achievement. Then it seemed to crumble: campus unrest, anti-Vietnam demonstrations, Nixon and Watergate and then withdrawal from Vietnam. Would the malaise extend to the sphere of business?

The summer of 1980 produced a resounding answer – in the pages of the *Harvard Business Review*. Two Harvard professors, Robert Hayes and William Abernathy, published an article under the provocative title 'Managing our Way to Economic Decline' (Hayes and Abernathy, 1980). This article began with a striking lack of ambiguity:

> During the past several years American business has experienced a marked deterioration of competitive vigour and a growing unease about its overall economic well being.

No pulling of punches here. And why should the USA be experiencing these difficulties? Because:

> Our experience suggests that, to an unprecedented degree, success in most industries today requires an organizational commitment to compete in the market place on technological grounds – that is, to compete over the long run by offering superior products.

As Hayes and Abernathy develop their thesis American companies are variously indicted for:

- short-termism
- declining R & D expenditure in the 1970s
- similarly, declining capital investment
- sluggish productivity growth over the period 1960–78 (the USA is bottom out of the 10 countries cited; Japan, of course, is top)
- excessive concern with marketing, and reliance on the power of marketing effort to 'shift produce'
- excessive promotion to top corporate posts of people with a finance and/or legal background, with a corresponding neglect of engineering
- a corresponding cult of 'hands off' pseudo-professionalism
- a preoccupation with mergers and acquisitions, at the expense of product development

This is some indictment for a country that 10 years earlier had been regarded as *the* economic superpower of all time. Hayes and Abernathy's treatise is stiffened by respectful references to German practice, and ends with an exemplary discussion of 'the European example'.

Before the year was out another salvo was fired, in the pages of the same journal, by another Harvard professor, Raymond Vernon (Vernon, 1990). Vernon's paper is entitled 'Gone are the Cash Cows of Yesteryear'. Vernon assembles a different thesis, but one that is complementary to that of Hayes and Abernathy. First he notes the inevitable erosion of America's superior wealth:

> The 1970s began to obliterate features that had distinguished the United States from other industrialized countries. For one thing, European and Japanese income levels were rising rapidly and no longer trailed far behind those of the Americans.

So why didn't American industry rush in to serve this growing demand? Because, in effect, it disqualified itself by an unworthy adherence to American norms:

> But their [American] innovations have differed from those of the Europeans in some important respects. In industrial goods, Europeans tended to stress innovation that would conserve capital and raw materials, such as the use of oxygen in blast furnaces and fuel injection in automobile motors. Americans tended to concentrate on labor saving innovations and these were profligate with energy and raw materials.

Or again:

> In consumer goods, the United States ground out a stream of new products that could satisfy an apparently unlimited appetite for novelty and comfort.

Whereas the more wholesome Europeans, of course, opted for smaller, more 'fuel efficient' and durable products, Vernon underlines the need for American manufacturers to produce goods that are likely to appeal to Europeans by being both cheaper and more durable. And indeed to take something, design ideas indeed as well as market intelligence, from their manufacturing outposts in Europe. Whereas in practice:

> The main task of subsidiaries (in Europe) is to convince the local populace that their (American) products are exactly what it wants.

This idea of adapting to other countries, rather than being dominant in them, is taken up again in the last chapter of this book in the light of our elaboration of the strengths and weaknesses of American management.

Systematising the thesis

While it is beyond our scene-setting purposes to engage in a detailed exploration of the decline thesis, there is another contribution to the literature that merits discussion here. This is a book that came out of the MIT Commission on Industrial Productivity at the end of the 1980s (Dertouzos *et al.*, 1989). This work systematises by taking a longer time perspective, by itemising the strengths and advantages enjoyed by the USA at the end of the Second World War and noting their inevitable erosion. Thus, at its simplest, the USA was the only major industrial economy undamaged by the war, but by definition this comparative strength could not last beyond a period of post-war reconstruction for victors and vanquished alike.

Dertouzos and his co-authors also give added substance to the relative decline thesis by looking in some detail at eight industries in the USA. These industry analyses are not all bad news, but there is a preponderance of bad news. The section on the machine tool industry, for instance, begins with the observation:

> The American machine tool industry collapsed in the early 1980s when imports surged just as demand slumped.

That on the steel industry begins:

> The American steel industry was once the largest, most modern, and most efficient in the world. From 1975–1985, however, it suffered declining demand for its products, loss of market share at home, falling production and unemployment, and low or negative earnings.

Or again writing of the semi-conductor, computer and copier industries:

> All three of these areas once seemed to be secure American preserves, but all these are now under attack by overseas challenges.

But the consumer-electronics industry is the nadir:

> Among the industries studied, consumer electronics provides the clearest illustration of an innovative high-growth industry that has been virtually eliminated in the United States by overseas competition.

In short, this testimony 'pulls no punches' yet perhaps it is some of the less declarative observations offered by the authors that are more revealing. In speaking of the automobile industry, for example, it is observed:

> Each worker or supplier was expected to do an assigned job but no one expected them to make any effort to improve the way the job was done.

A reflection that reveals a rather mechanical approach to work organisation, perhaps acceptable in the days of impersonal systems designed by industrial engineers to obtain efficiencies with big numbers.

In the discussion of the civil aviation industry the authors remark that times have changed; technical performance and product support are no longer enough since competition has expanded to include a variety of financial and political factors. The suggestion seems to be that American manufacturers are less than adequately sensitive to these new factors and are, as it were, still playing yesterday's winning hand.

Or referring to the textile industry: 'A narrow focus on keeping wages low and fighting unionisation has also been central to competitive strategy.'

Again the suggestion is, should it have been, or were these measures no more than defensive?

Finally, in the discussion of the machine tool industry, the authors quote a General Motors executive:

> If you buy the very best from Japan, it has already been in Toyota Motors for two years, and if you buy from West Germany, it has already been with BMW for a year and a half.

This hints of a cooperation, a symbiosis in some of America's trade rivals, not typical of the USA itself. Or as Lester Thurow (1992) would have it, Germany and Japan are exemplars of a communitarian capitalism that departs from the classic American formulation of market forces, competition and results. And these departures arguably endow those states with the advantage of playing to different rules.

Economy or decline

The middle part of this chapter sketched the scale and substance of the American economy: the last few pages have dipped into the literature on decline. This raises the simple question, which is preponderant? What is the balance that the reader should take away?

For several reasons, it is the scale and substance of the American economy that matters more. First of all, the decline posited in the literature is a relative decline. Relative in the sense of a comparison with other countries, of course. The countries chosen for this comparison are invariably Germany and Japan, but these are the superstars of the later twentieth century. A comparison with Britain and France would not be so humbling. The decline is also relative in the sense of a comparison with America's own immediate post-war past. Here again some measure of decline was quite inescapable. At

Table 2.4

Country	per capita dollars
USA	22,204
Switzerland	21,747
Luxembourg	21,372
Germany	19,500
Canada	19,178
Japan	19,107

Source: *US Statistical Abstract*, 1994

the end of the Second World War the USA was not only a mighty economic player, but in the first few years virtually the only player.

Second, not only is the decline relative, but it is primarily an economic phenomenon. There is no suggestion that the USA has lost Great Power status even if it has lost economic leadership. Indeed its Great Power status, and ideological rectitude, was enhanced by the fall of European communism.

Third, America does have, and does appear to be using, the option of compensating for loss of competitiveness in manufactured goods in some branches of industry with exports based on natural resources. Michael Porter is doubtless right to see this as a cause for concern, but at least the USA *has* its natural resources. Consider that this would not be an option for Germany, still less Japan, if these countries were to lose their edge in manufacturing.

Indeed this nexus of argument is put very nicely by Porter (1990b) following his analysis of developments in the USA after the golden age of post-war supremacy:

> America is no repeat of the British story and is in little danger of losing its status as a major power. America's size, natural resources and breadth of industries effectively preclude that.

And indeed Americans might take comfort from comparative wealth figures. The 1994 *US Statistical Abstract* shows the USA as having a relatively high GND per capita for 1991. But, the USA is surpassed on this measure by several countries, including Norway, Sweden, Denmark, Finland, Switzerland and Japan. Evidence of relative decline? No, two pages on, the same source gives GDP per capita using purchasing power parities. How it comes out for the top six in 1991 is shown in Table 2.4.

I would like to round off this scene-setting chapter on a note that is both more speculative and less crassly materialistic! South-East Asia has attracted interest and attention as an economic growth area, and since the end of 1989 there has been much speculation about the likely fate of the East European countries as well. I have no quarrel with either judgement, but would like to suggest that the potential of Latin America may have been overlooked. So far the 1990s have been a time of hope, and relatively speaking, a time of peace for the Latin American sub-continent. If there is a surge of economic development, and particularly of consumer demand, the USA is bound to be the main external beneficiary.

It is difficult to 'factor in' imponderables of this kind to sober analyses of relative economic standing, but they may be decisive.

3

Individualism

> American officers and men gave a practical lesson in equality
> by their familiarity with each other and by their mutual respect.
> They impressed Marburgers by their individualism, both in acts
> of kindness and in crime and corruption. Above all, Americans
> seemed to get things done
>
> John Gimbel

Marburg is a university town in Germany, north-east of Frankfurt
am Main. John Gimbel is an historian writing about the American
occupation of this community in the period right after the Second
World War. Gimbel is American, and it is interesting to see that he
picks out individualism as an American feature that will strike the
Germans, and that he links it with equality and accomplishment.
But most of all Gimbel is remarkable for his idiosyncratic view of
how this individualism may be expressed – an example we will try
to follow in the present chapter.

Praise in management

The concern in this chapter of course is with the role and manifestation of individualism in management rather than in the wider
society, even if we make occasional reference to the latter. In the
management context Americans do not praise the individual for
being a friction-free part in a well oiled machine. You never hear
praise along the lines of 'Ann fits in so well you'd never know she
was here', or, 'Rod is such a great team player he doesn't stand out
at all'. When individuals are praised it is for qualities that differentiate them not integrate them. They are picked out and lauded for
having qualities that are in relatively short supply, and for having
them to a high degree. So the individual is praised for being forceful,
charismatic, having great energy and drive, being smarter than the
rest, being ahead of the pack. The consistency with which it occurs
underlines a deep American commitment to individualism, to differentiating achievement by individuals.

Consider a few examples. Here is the head of a largely independent operating company describing the overall boss at group
headquarters:

He has taken the company from 31 million to 1.6 billion. He is chairman as well as CEO [chief executive officer]. He is larger than life, he is a legend.

Here is vice-president of another company, referring to the deputy CEO, his boss: 'He is very intense and hands on.' Note that 'tense' and 'intense' may be used as terms of praise in America, but never in Britain, where they would denote a lack of balance or of proportion. The speaker in this case went on to an anecdote concerning an old and trusted employee who failed to get to work because his old and unreliable car packed up. The 'hands on' deputy CEO told a personnel manager to take the employee out and buy him a car! The story ended with the observation: 'When Pete wants something done he wants it done.'

Or consider the case of another medium-sized company that is about to take over a smaller company in another state. The executive team are discussing the fate of the employees at the acquired company, many of whom they will let go, but there are some exceptions. They discuss the woman at the smaller company who runs the MIS (management information systems); the MIS boss of the acquiring company is not present, but one of his colleagues reports: 'I told him she has some pluses and a few minuses. He's going to take her, she's a real go-getter!'

One of the fascinating things about America from a British standpoint is the way drive, energy and the ability to get things done (shake things up) is presumed to be a good thing. In another company visited, the deputy MHR (management of human resources) chief spoke with manifest approbation of a younger colleague on another site, saying: 'She's a real mover and shaker.' Now even if 'mover and shaker' were a standard expression in Britain, which it is not, one would be very cautious about handing out this accolade. British listeners might well react by asking themselves, whose toes is she treading on, how many important people has she upset, how badly has she rocked the boat, and has she provoked a wildcat strike yet?

A company in the South-west has taken over another company in the North. They plan to take the MHR vice-president from the acquired company and move her into the top MHR post in one of their divisions. But her fame has preceded her, and she apparently has something of a 'black prince' reputation. The MHR vice-president at the headquarters of the acquiring company tells his team about the impending transfer, but it does not go unchallenged:

Subordinate: There is a story that when the workers up in Omaha heard she was leaving they turned off their machines and cheered.
Vice-president: I heard she kept the union out of there single-handed.

In other words it is corporate achievement that counts, not cheap popularity. The MHR vice-president goes on to enumerate her strengths, which include:

a law degree
the fact that she is known to work 60 hours a week
'she's kind of intense'

Note again 'intense' as a term of praise. Also the idea that long hours of work are *ipso facto* a sign of merit and quality – a presumption that would not go unchallenged in Britain. The subordinate has one more go:

Subordinate: They say she looks like Olive Oyl.
Vice-president: I don't care about that. The tall blonde we had in medical division didn't do so well.

The individual self-depicts

A variation on the theme explored so far of managers lauded by their colleagues for larger-than-life personalities is the way individual managers depict themselves. How much more satisfactory to praise yourself and eliminate all possibility of error (or undersell).

One entrepreneur interviewed by the author in Texas, who had founded an electrical repair business in the aftermath of the Second World War, was moved to consider the issue of corporate succession:

You have to lead not push. My son wants to take over, but he is too idle. I don't send people out to do repairs I can't do myself. I know I neglect my family to a considerable extent by being that way. I am strictly a leader.

Another entrepreneur, this time from Dayton, Ohio, saw opportunity mixed with *noblesse oblige*:

By the time you are over 40 you have had some favours, and it is time to put something back. This is about facilitating 'the American Dream'. I try to get that philosophy across. My father was always on about it. He always said that anyone could become President.

The self-depiction is not necessarily about seeing oneself as better; it may be a matter of interpreting and then acting out the spirit of the nation, as in the previous example. Another possibility is individual differentiation by commitment. The president of an agricultural cooperative in Texas put it this way:

Well, I got on because I liked what I was doing, I was willing to do more than was expected of me. I did not have an attitude of 'I'm not going to do that, I don't get paid for it'.

But a bit of self-assurance never comes amiss. Here is the operations vice-president of a building materials company in the Middle West, asked by the author about job satisfaction:

> I love it! I like to make decisions. You ask me a question, I give you an answer. I'm right most of the time, that's why I'm here. I got good street smartness.

The importance of control is conflated with individual autonomy. Where one has the capability to control there can be no shirking the issue. Here is the manufacturing vice-president of a consumer products company in the mid-South, addressing a meeting of his subordinates. They source a semi-manufactured component from Mexico; cheap of course, but not always reliable:

> but what I have is a serious problem with damaged parts, and we have to address it. Some of it seems to be Mexican imports. But I will simply not put up with it – we'll get new Mexicans if we have to.

And a little bit later:

> That brings us to domestic issues which you guys have to address. These are areas where we do have control, and we must get control up.

In other words we are not here to let things happen to us: we are here to make things happen for us. And, of course, the more important an individual the more important it will be for even more senior people to control him or her. Here is the president of an insurance company asked by the author about outside contacts. Before mentioning auditors, consultants, lawyers, the industry association, and so on he replies: 'With the parent company in Houston, almost daily by phone.' Or again the CEO of an American-owned publishing company in Britain: 'I am controlled every minute of the day by New Jersey [company headquarters]. It's hot in this here kitchen!'

My point across the last few examples is not that managers in the USA are more vainglorious than their counterparts in other countries. It is rather that their answers take the individual to be pivotal: he or she is brighter or righter, more committed, more controlled or controlling.

Career and individualism

Careerism, of course, is not exclusive to the United States. I would like to suggest, however, that it is more overt in that country. More overt, less restrained, more uncompromising, more taken for granted. Keep in mind here that careerism and individualism go hand in hand; only individuals can have careers. A career is a measure of individual worth in which a single person's occupational achievement is evaluated in context and against a time dimension, along the lines of: how far did he or she get, what was the magnitude of the achievement, what were the obstacles, and how long did it take? Consider one or two examples.

Here is the operations vice-president quoted earlier as being right 'most of the time'. This manager completed High School. His father worked as a house painter. This manager began work in a factory, a manual job, 'bunching up track for garage doors'. He moved in the same plant to a job in production control (devising and monitoring production schedules), then to a job in purchasing (buying the components and materials for the manufacturing programme), and then to an office job, still in the same company, for getting on for 10 years. Then the company is swept away by a series of mergers, the manager concerned goes back to the purchasing function and ends up as director of purchasing. Then he moves to his present employer, as a buyer, and works his way up to vice-president of purchasing; this in turn is followed by a lateral move to vice-president operations (more responsibility, more subordinates).

Note some of the ingredients here. 'Completed High School' and 'father worked as a house painter' equals not college educated and not born with a silver spoon in his mouth. As the manager comments: 'I made a lot of my own luck!'

And note the role of mergers. Whenever you ask middle-aged American managers to talk about their careers there is a good chance that mergers and acquisitions will come up, leading variously to redundancy, geographic transfer, movement to a new type of work, sometimes to enhanced opportunity. In the case just cited a larger employing organisation, probably with more formalised management, sees the manager's potential and puts him on a job track that takes him up to director of purchasing. By this time the manager concerned has both the confidence and marketability to strike out on his own and move to his present company. His final comment was: 'My boss says he made me. But I tell him, I've always been a feather in your cap.'

Here is a different theme, this time from a university-educated executive vice-president of a company making a technically sophisticated consumer product distributed via specialist dealers and agents; agent efficiency is pretty important:

> I've been with the company for 30 years. I finished High School, went to College – electrical engineering degree. Then to graduate school specialising in colour TV, standards and design. Then I came here.
>
> I was brought in by the executive sponsor. I didn't like the interviewer much, a bean counter. I was placed in a one man research department. We expanded. I moved into engineering, engineering in the sense of the

link between R & D [research and development] and production. I became head of engineering, and then director of the whole of engineering plus R & D.

Then I became director of operations, plus R & D and engineering. Then I was made PA to the president. I got into marketing from this assignment. In fact there is a lot of technique in this. I found a way to evaluate dealers' efficiency with a 7 parameter model; that is to say, you can tell what the sales should be, down to each zip code! I brought the power of statistics. Like you are trying to get information out of noise.

A one-company career, but a fascinating testimony. First we have the role of company expansion, without which this manager might have languished in his one-man research department. Anyone who is middle-aged towards the end of the century is likely to have benefited from the unprecedented expansion of the world economy in the 1950s and 1960s – and the older they are the more they are likely to have benefited. Second, note the internal mobility, the movement across departments or functions – research, engineering, operations, PA-ship, marketing. This kind of versatility-mobility is more pronounced in the USA than in Continental Europe. Third, the passage quoted above from the interview notes is redolent with the American conviction: it is not what you know but what you can do with it that counts. Evaluate dealer efficiency with a 7 parameter model, *down to each zip code* – now you're talking, man.

Here is a different testimony, from a woman in a HRM (human resource management) post in a key city public transport authority (PTA):

I've been here 20 years
It's the only job I have had
I started working here while at college
Started as a file clerk
PTA had a graduate training programme: before it had only been for men, but I talked myself into it

Time and time again in talking to these managers, their first contact with a corporate employer or an industry had been the result of working while at college. For the most part they are referring to college employment experiences in the 1950s, 1960s or 1970s; working while at college has become more common in Europe, but it started earlier (was always the norm) in the USA and occurs on a much larger scale. For many college-educated Americans it served to unite the world of work and a sense of its opportunities and practicalities with the higher education experience – something which is more often the object of contrivance in Europe.

The fact of this manager getting on to a graduate training programme, in spite of being a woman, will have occurred probably in the late 1960s. For the most part this battle has been won. A European visiting American companies is likely to be struck by the prevalence of women managers, and the fact that they are less obviously concentrated in traditional female slots – in industries such as retailing and publishing, for example, or in the personnel function. And at least in some ways they seem to be treated in the same way as are the men. Consider a practical example. A manager in a company in Philadelphia who needs to send a woman subordinate on a trouble-shooting trip to a plant in Kansas City, will just send her. It will be assumed that she can 'look after herself', and handle hotels, airports and car hire (car hire is an indispensable part of business trips in the USA). Now if one can imagine this scenario in say Britain, France or Switzerland, the male manager doing the picking and sending might hesitate in an old-fashioned protective way: is it fair to send a woman, can she cope with two nights away from home, what will her husband think?

There is a broader issue. Part of the burden of this book is that there are some recurring elements of disposition and behaviour that make up a recognisable American style in management. If you meet women managers in American companies, listen to their dialogue, see their role in group discussions, their contribution to meetings, their priorities and *modus operandi* seem to be the same as that of their male colleagues. They are part of American management style, not a sub-set or alternative.

Career and mobility

A few of the American managers I talked to in the course of the study had worked for only one company or employing organisation, and I have introduced examples of this *genre* already. But rather more of them have had a succession of employers, sometimes adding geographic mobility to mobility between companies.

To begin with here is the vice-president administration of a Middle Western company producing and distributing bottled water:

> After high school I was in the army, and served in Korea. Came back in 1952, and went to college on the GI Bill. In the summer I worked for Pepsi as a route salesman. The next vac. I worked for Perrier's own water business; stayed with the company for 15 years.
>
> I became their assistant controller. Then the company survived a hostile takeover, and the president organised a 'white knight' rescue by Coke. Found I was placed with a load of younger people. So I went as controller into the automobile business: set up finance, leasing, insurance companies. It was interesting experience. Then came the 1973 fuel crash. Then I went to an engineering firm as a senior project accountant, in

charge of all their projects in the Middle East. I went with them to California to work on field projects; I also got experience of purchasing materials, of payroll, and more besides. Got an MBA as well. Then in 1984 I was head-hunted here to Vice President.

In its way this testimony is an American idyll, where the themes include:

- for the older generation, military service and the GI Bill
- first contact with the industry as a result of vacation employment
- mobility and versatility: soft drinks, auto-industry, engineering, back to drinks
- geographic mobility, down to California, and back to the Middle West
- an MBA 'on the hoof'
- being head-hunted, the natural consequence of merit

Let us stand back for a moment, and consider this existentially. The question of mobility is relevant to the theme of individualism, because of relative constancy. There is the individual, and there is where he or she is. If the place gets varied, becomes temporary, emerges as the dependent variable, then it is the individual who is constant, who is the only continuity in a flux of a circumstantial change, who achieves an enhanced reality.

Here is another example, the president of the insurance company already cited:

I graduated from high school in Gary, Indiana. My father worked in the steel mills. I went to a private, RC, all-male college to please my parents. I had to borrow money. It was a small liberal arts college. I developed the work ethic there, and did a BA in Economics.

Straight away we have some now familiar themes. Gary, Indiana signifies a non-privileged start in life – it was, after all, murder capital USA in 1993! Father working in the steel mills pushes the message home. Then comes the Protestant Ethic. All-male, RC liberal arts college; does not sound a lot of fun – maybe not, but one learned the work ethic, and there is no substitute for that.

The story continues:

After graduation, first job in an insurance company in Indiana, as an underwriter approving applications for insurance. And they transferred me to Georgia; by this time I was married with two children and 'starving to death', so I looked around. So my third move was to a new insurance company in the mid-South. But they were bought by another company, headquartered in Texas. I left to join another company in Kentucky, and became vice-president. Stayed with them for two years. Then the Texas based company invited me back to Dallas. I was with their life insurance company and moved between the operating company and the holding company. In this period I was exposed to everything:

- mergers
- selling companies
- product design
- compensation plans

Then I came to the Mid-South company as president-COO [Chief Operating Officer]. After that they moved me to another subsidiary company in Florida as CEO. Then back here to the mid-South as president-CEO.

This was one of the first interviews in the series. Given the whirlpool of geographic and corporate moves it seemed natural to ask if this were at all out of the ordinary. The laconic reply was that the whole thing was: 'Not too unusual.' Perhaps he is right. Here is a MHR vice-president at a consumer goods company in the South:

I started out in a West Pennsylvania steel town. I was a good football player and I got a football scholarship to college. Then as a graduate I joined a steel company as an operations trainee. Then came the army, and two years as a lieutenant. Then back to the steel company, but this time into personnel to run college relations (i.e. graduate recruiting). There I was transferred to a mill in Cleveland, Ohio, where I was in charge of training and employment; I had eight years there.

I left to go to three other companies in succession to serve as director of personnel. I came here to the South as vice-president of another company. But then I got to know someone who worked for the Greyhound Corporation in Phoenix; he recruited me as vice-president. But then our president left Greyhound to become president of another company; he took me with him, and I became CEO and president of hotel operations, and ran it for the Japanese. Then I went to another company in Phoenix, a lumber company, as MHR vice-president. But this company was acquired, they fired all of us [executives] so I came here to this company in the South as HR vice president. I have done 100 contracts [with labour unions] in my time. Sure, I worked for eight companies.

Here we have the complete mobility package. Social mobility (West Pennsylvania steel town designates humble beginnings, from which the football scholarship is the first escape), mobility between companies, geographic mobility (Pennsylvania to Ohio to Arizona, crossed with in and out of the South), a variety of industries, and with merger–acquisition–redundancy playing a part in the story.

Anyone with these experiences is bound to be robust, proactive, proud of their achievement. This is clearly the case with the executive whose career has just been outlined. In the USA labour contracts are negotiated at plant and/or company level, not at industry level, and in a decent-sized company this task will fall to the HR boss. These contracts are important, and the whole operation is more hard-hitting and explicitly play-to-win than in any of the European countries, including Britain. If the employees have an advantage they will certainly press it. If they do not get what they want they will strike; if this happens it is understood that management will fight back – will attempt to run the plant with managers and non-union white-collar employees; they will bring in 'new hires' if they have a chance, and about to strike employees will engage in pre-emptive sabotage if they have a chance. To have negotiated 100 such contracts is some record: this is executive macho American style.

Individualism and success

Central to American individualism is the importance attached to success. The presumption is that individuals will naturally strive for success and will not be happy until the success has been achieved. This is, at least in degree, a distinctive feature of American society. And it is not something that goes without saying or something that follows inevitably from the premise of individualism. Heightened individualism might well lead to an enhanced emphasis on adjustment, fulfilment, interiority, or a refined and differentiated consciousness. Now these values are not, of course, absent from American society, but they are not primary. In first place is success, and success has to be worldly and visible. Success for most is high rank and high income: when you have achieved these there is no doubt about it, in your eyes or anyone else's. And there are other twists to the American–European comparison which I will try to illustrate.

Here is a senior vice president of a major company reviewing his career. He left High School and went to a minor university in his home state. There are two themes here: local loyalty (a southerner and proud of it), and the common putting down a marker on humble origins – anything achieved is real success for the individual, not the effortless product of a privileged start in life. On graduation this manager joins a retail chain as a management trainee, actually working on the shop floor. He becomes the personnel manager of one of the stores, and then personnel manager at the corporate headquarters. Then a move to a larger retailer as MHR director for the chain's largest franchisee. Then MHR – director of the whole operation, then MHR vice president, and then senior vice president at national headquarters. But this is just the bare bones and there are some stories.

Manager: In my first company I looked in the phone book and saw there were some posts with no names against them, including a personnel job. I reckoned I would make an impact in personnel in this industry, so I called head office and asked. They said yes it is a vacancy, and you can have it if you want it, but it's in Jackson, Mississippi. I said straight away: 'I'll go to Mississippi'.

Author: What's wrong with Jackson?

Manager: It's a long way from anywhere, it's hot, and you can see the steam coming off the sidewalk!

Two years later he is about to buy a house in Jackson, asks first and is told, go ahead – you won't be moved. He bought the house. Then immediately he was offered an opening in the corporate head office. He took it (none of this European-style wimpish nonsense about children changing schools and wives having to make new friends). But we are not through yet. What brought this manager to his second company was a personnel/MHR post in which Equal Employment Opportunity Commission (EEOC) work was critical. When he applied the manager claimed to be an EEOC expert, though he was not. But before the interview he read it up ('I worked my butt off'). When he got the job he decided to watch the EEOC lawyers at work, saying, 'I want to see you guys are doing it right.' In this way he got a feel and understanding for EEOC work, and came to be able to do it pretty well. He ended up as the industry EEOC expert, and proud of it.

Note the alert opportunism in this story: looking for opportunities, being proactive, making your own luck. Then there is the instant readiness to make sacrifices for the sake of career advance. Jackson, Mississippi may not be your ideal posting, but if that is where the opportunity is . . . It may be a lot of hassle to sell a house you have only just bought, but we are not going to throw away the chance to get to the corporate head office.

But there is also the amoral tinge. The account seems to say: so I told lies on the application form; so what, I justified it by reading up afterwards, didn't I? So I managed to get a job I couldn't actually do; well with a bit of bluff I figured a way to get on top of it. I succeeded, I am an expert now, who is going to quibble?

I do not mean to suggest that American managers typically do vastly evil things on the way up. The implied comparison with Europe is not black and white, it is in pastel shades, but it is real for all that. In the American case:

- success is more likely to be defined in worldly terms
- its pursuit is more open, more readily acknowledged, no one has to pretend that 'they are not really trying'

- if you have to break the rules, play a thin hand with audacity, cut a few corners, well, nobody is going to remember so long as you pull it off

In the American scheme of things, success is its own justification. One of the interviewed executives was asked about the relative prestige of his function, and promptly answered in salary terms pointing out that he was the sixth most highly paid person in the whole organisation (listing the other five in order). He indicated his (truly impressive) executive suite with a magisterial sweep of the hand and concluded, 'I ended up in this room next to the president!'

A society that does not doubt itself has strengths indeed.

4

Strategy

The Americans invented business strategy.

While business strategy like management itself, may have been practised by business leaders in other places and at other times, it is the Americans who developed a consciousness of strategy, articulated it, and prioritised it. The Americans are pre-eminent in strategy consultancy, they dominate the research literature, and indeed there are few non-American strategy textbooks. As a quick litmus test consider that when Moore published his neat little book *Writers on Strategy and Strategic Management* (1992) purporting to review in brief the contributions of leading strategy thinkers, 30 out of the 32 whose work he discusses were American (the remaining two were English speaking: a Briton with a Stanford MBA and a Canadian from Montreal). Nor is there any special pleading about this selection; Moore himself is British, though with American credentials, and so is the publisher – Penguin.

Is there a reason why strategy should be an American inspiration? I would like to suggest that it is the product of desire crossed with capability.

Histories of America tend to stress the thousands of people who went there in the seventeenth and eighteenth centuries seeking religious and political freedom. This is not contested, but instead I would emphasise the millions of immigrants in the nineteenth and twentieth centuries who went to the USA in the expectation of material improvement. Is it any wonder that the USA became the most *explicitly* materialistic society, where goals of personal enrichment are universally accepted and lauded? Where success, fulfilment, and even happiness may be meaningfully 'dollarised'.

Side by side with the strong attachment to wealth achievement are the natural advantages enjoyed by American corporations. They are bigger than those of most other countries; they have the biggest (and richest) domestic market; they 'went international' decades earlier than the leading companies of most other countries. They are the best placed to exploit economies of scale; to achieve market dominance; and to impose their will, their products and their *modus operandi* beyond the national borders. This is claiming a good deal.

If one crosses the desire for money-making with the corporate capability then an enhanced concern with business strategy is a natural consequence. What is strategy, after all, if not a set of programmatic rationalisations for the achievement of *future* corporate prosperity.

The mechanics of corporate strategy also both play to and express a further collection of American strengths. While strategy is not about information, it is driven by information, and this information gathering and collation, as I have shown earlier, is an American forte. What is more, a lot of the conceptual apparatus of business strategy – market share, market dominance, scale and scope, competitive advantage, differentiation, segmentation, and so on – are systematising concepts. They take a basic notion, that is to say, and then 'break it down', grade it, classify it, relativise it, and show where it is going. These action typologies are distinctively American: not philosophic enough to attract the Germans, not clever enough for the French, and too self-consciously serious for the British.

The argument about strategy that we are developing here centres primarily on a difference of degree. It is not that business strategy has found no acceptance elsewhere, but rather that its espousal is stronger, more central, and less equivocal in American companies. I once interviewed the chief executive of a leading company in Sweden and put to him an open-ended question about the nature of his job. This evoked the reply: 'It's all fire-fighting, really.'

Now such a reply would be unthinkable from an American in the equivalent position. The fire-fighting element – the crisis handling, solving current problems, removing 'road-blocks', dealing with operational contingencies – would be recognised. Indeed the American executive would face up to some of that as well, but the emphasis would be on the thinking, shaping, planning, directing of the enterprise: in short, upon strategic issues.

Strategy and the managers

The starting point for the American managers' concern with strategy is that whatever entity you are in charge of, whatever the legal or organisational status, it is a business really – something that will be accountable and must be profitable. Here is a MHR vice-president of an air frame manufacturer setting the scene for the author:

> We are a division of ABC and a subsidiary of XYZ but we act independently and have our own P & L Account. We really are running a business here.

Like American nationalism, being *in business* is as much a matter of emotional conviction as it is of formal reality. The strategic imperative follows from this conviction. And since strategy is the first duty of the business leader it has to be exercised up-front and from the start. Here is the CEO of a footwear company reconstructing for the author his first moves on appointment:

> I joined the corporation 3 years ago. It was very healthy, it was growing. But it was selling footwear that was like everyone else's, and it was selling on price. So I set out as a personal mission; well, I wasn't interested in chasing sales and produce. So I used the theme:
>
>> comfort through technology
>> product differentiation
>> and moderate rather than low price
>
> OK, we still make a lot of what we used to make. But anything that we do has to be measured against our mission statement.

Are this executive's few words not a marvellous encapsulation of the strategic imperative? You come in with your eyes open, and you act dispassionate. Sure the company may be making money, but how? By selling a million and making a dollar on each? Well, we don't want to be busy fools do we, better to be idle rich. And the company is growing, sure, but how? By chasing high-volume, low-margin sales. Well that growth will not be sustainable if we are doing the same thing as everyone else. So resolve to develop a conscious mission. Use manufacturing technique, and no doubt fashion design and advertising, to create the fact (or image) of different products, different from everyone else's. Now you can grow, and that is sustainable, and you can charge higher prices. And now you have criteria with which to assess the product range and the performance of individual items.

Here is another chief executive, this time the head of a mechanical engineering company making consumer products supplied to retailers. He reacts to an open-ended question from the author about how he sees his CEO role, making three points. For this executive the priorities are:

- strategic direction
- picking good people and letting them get on with it
- getting involved with customers when the individual customer is big enough; with big customers, the cost of error is bigger

Developing the first priority, strategic direction, this executive says that the essence of it is:

> To understand customer needs.
> To use our flexibility to make ourselves more valuable to the market. We can increase the risk for retailers of holding imports (i.e. products from foreign rivals) by moving fast from design to manufacture, by shipping

(i.e. delivering) on time and holding lots of inventory (so one can respond instantly to any request).

Note the thinking. It is a battlefield. We have to win the customer and defeat the enemy. To achieve these 'war aims' we will deploy our competitive weapon – the manufacturing facility. We can initiate frequent design changes (the product is a semi-fashion item) and follow this through by getting the new models into production quickly, and then delivering consignments promptly. All this will please customers/end-users and they will like the new models. The retailers will like getting fashionably saleable models promptly, as well as being able to replenish stocks from company inventory. At the same time the foreign imports are undermined, marginalised, rendered just that little bit less fashionable (and appealing) and the retailer is gently punished for having allowed these cuckoos into the nest.

A variation on the theme is to say that American executives typically show a strong industry knowledge; this is rather less to be taken for granted than it might be in Europe when one remembers the often high levels of individual manager mobility, between companies and industries, illustrated in the last chapter. What is more, this industry knowledge is typically expressed in a quantitative way – and pithily. Here is the chief executive of a stationery company:

> This industry is a 2.5 billion dollar business. There are about 200 manufacturers. Some supply end-users, some feed into a distribution system. It is very concentrated among the top five, then very fragmented. We are in the top five. The top five share 40% of sales.

As we saw with the chief executive of the footwear company, the American strategist goes in and makes a strategic appraisal fast. Here is the owner of a health care system company in the South-West. When he bought the company it was primarily renting domestic servants short term but had a minor health care services provision facility:

> Maids Inc. was primarily a maid service for [a posh residential area of the city concerned]. People there wanted less than a full-time maid, just a few hours now and again, paying premium rates. Maids Inc. also ran an assistance programme for elderly people for the City authority. The former owners of Maids Inc. had never been much interested in the support for the elderly part – they did not see it as a source of profit, just as a subsidy. It was not profitable because of the way they had set up the contract; I turned it off in 30 days.

Note the pattern. The newly sworn-in sheriff rides into town, takes stock, sees two parts, one is underexploited, he figures out why, and takes swift and decisive action. The hard-ball player then gets his reward, as we see:

> The City authority responded, begging me to keep the contract going (no one else wanted to service this contract). The City waived all the rules, and gave me a 25% rise. I should say, my background is marketing, and I have an MBA from North Western. I studied the market and the demographic trends: there would be more and more people needing and qualifying for the elderly care program.

Note the development here. The new owner identifies a potentially profitable operation, neglected by the previous owners, and gets the contract price raised. But there is more than this. The owner identifies not just a profitable niche, but a *growing* demand. The next stage is to gear the company up to exploit this advantage:

> We felt we could appeal to the customer as a commercial operation, not just as an administrative referral system. We provided service within 24 hours, not the statutory 72 hours; sometimes we responded in a couple of hours.

As with the mechanical engineering company discussed a little earlier, the organisation itself serves as the competitive weapon. It differentiates itself from potential rivals by being fast, flexible and responsive. This posture naturally brings its reward:

> We got a reputation, got more referrals. We went outside the city and outside the state. Then we felt we could go nationwide. We were looking at it as a business. We listened to client complaints, and we responded to these.

These American strategy formulations also tend to be dynamic in the sense of indicating change over time, response to environmental change, or whatever. The CEO of the insurance company, cited in the last chapter as an example of amazing career mobility, offers a neat example in his succinct response to an open-ended question about strategy:

> We are the result of a merger. I used to be the president of one of the merged companies. Our strategy now is to concentrate on the growth of premiums, not upon efficiency as in the past through consolidation based upon mergers. We are doing this by increasing the number of agents; we are now growing the agents ón a managed and controlled basis.

Simple isn't it? First merge, grow big, achieve economies of scale, then rationalise, reduce the cost structure, and raise margins. Then when this strategy has been pushed to its conclusion, put (controlled and managed) resources into the sales operation to expand premium revenue, and raise profits.

I am not suggesting that strategic thinking is unique to American companies. The implied contrast is rather one of degree and prevalence. American companies always seem to have a conscious strategy; it is always explicit, not implicit; people can always articulate it for you – typically in the succinct and focused way illustrated in the last few pages. Another feature of these strategic pronouncements is that they are seldom clouded by sentiment. As the ultimate example here again is the CEO of the stationery company:

> If some of the things I've talked about happen, a key decision will be when to exit this industry

Finally on the theme of the prevalence of strategy consider this contribution from the president of one of the smaller companies in the sample. This is a second generation family business in the Deep South employing 700 people across a number of manufacturing sites. The company makes a number of wire products: shelves and racks, lightning conductors, display equipment for shops, and so on. In response to the author's question about strategy the president replies:

> Well, we don't have well-defined business plans. Each kind of market has its own strategy. Each one has a different strategy. From our corporate group perspective we can see some that have better prospects than others, so we are trying to take cash from cash cows and give it to rising stars (but they get confused with dogs!). We aim at a maximum 10% growth per year. Sometimes we acquire a smaller competitor.

Now for all the humility and wry humour with which this is expressed, it has some substance:

- first, the recognition that the markets for the company's various products are different. This idea that companies may not have an overall strategy, but segment-specific strategies where a segment is a discrete product-market, is actually quite sophisticated; there are plenty of European companies of this size who are a long way from such a realisation
- the company has a reallocative policy, loosely based on the BCG (Boston Consulting Group) matrix
- there are growth targets
- there is an acquisitions policy
- and there is clearly an internal information system to support all this

Not a bad formulation for an owner-manager who is not really trying!

Industry developments

This ability to develop and explicate strategy seems to be embedded in a generally high level of awareness of industry, developments, problems and context. Again no black and white contrast with Europe is implied in this matter; it is rather that the American executives I interviewed uniformly showed high industry and context awareness, and could typically communicate this in an organised and focused way.

I have already cited an example of succinctly presented industry knowledge, from the chief executive of the stationery company. A variation on this theme is the readiness of these executives to give interesting answers to questions about developments in the industry. Here is a senior vice-president of a chain of departmental stores reflecting on what is going on in the industry:

> Among departmental stores you have bankruptcies and mergers. Marshall Field is being merged, for example. There is a whole re-positioning of the top tier.
>
> At the bottom there is 'gobbling up' by Target, K-Mart, and Wall-Mart. By the year 2000 it will be these three, plus a few mom and pop stores.
>
> In between you have layers of specialisation; this is very dynamic as needs are changing. We are doing this by having stores within a store; for example 'boutiques' for electrical goods or for car accessories. The speciality stores have expertise; but if consumer needs change there is nowhere for them to go.

How is that for a three-paragraph exposé of trends in American retailing together with a justification of the company's own strategy? Or another example, this time taken from an interview with the senior vice-president of a company that owns, edits and distributes a clutch of business magazines. Asked about industry developments, this executive argues that there are two:

> internationalisation
> segmentation

but that the two developments are if you like paradoxical. The internationalisation represents the spreading of the magazines across international boundaries, so that for example a Japanese version, an Australian version, a Korean version emerge. Yet side by side with this there is segmentation in the sense of a desire by the operators, driven by the needs of advertisers, to segment readership groups both between and within countries. Or put into other words, it is a move towards database marketing leading to readership segmentation, where this group gets this version of the magazine *with their adverts* and to a lesser extent their copy, and another group gets something else:

> It starts with the accumulation of data via credit cards. For instance I have a summer house in Wisconsin, I got a fishing licence (and pay for it by credit card) and in consequence get mail from fishing tackle companies. Everyone can get information on any segment, like Chicago dog owners!

It may be felt by readers that not very much is being claimed here, that surely senior operatives in any country will be able to speak about such industry developments with knowledge and discernment. Not so, in the author's experience. When you put this question to European managers you may well get a flood of questions back: what do you mean exactly, do you mean changes in manufacturing methods, or in consumer demand, or in pricing policy, or in government regulation? Now while such a questioning response is perfectly legitimate, it also in a way begs the question. When you ask what are the key industry developments you want to know what they think, you want to buy into their judgement as well as their knowledge. So it is up to them to decide whether to talk about technological change or the repositioning of major players within the industry. Americans usually give you the impression they ask themselves the question long before you ask it, and their response at that point of time is an act of communication not evaluation. It is the same with Key Success Factors.

Key Success Factors

The notion of Key Success Factors (KSFs) expresses the idea that for any particular company in any given industry there will be some things, the KSFs, that it must do well to survive, prosper, and hold its own against the competition. Now Americans can usually be relied upon to respond promptly and with discrimination to questions about KSFs.

Here as a starter illustration is the CEO of a company making primarily boxed chocolates, chocolate assortments and truffle chocolates. His answer emphasised the following considerations.

- selling fresh produce: note that this is a real policy choice; selling fresh means short shelf life, shorter production runs, logistical imperatives, a temporal quality control, and scrapping or discounting produce approaching its sell-by date
- locations in the sense of type of location of retail outlet: this is a company producing a top of the market quality product, comparable to say Godiva in Belgium; the retail outlets are to

reflect this in style and location. This company is represented for instance in the fashionable Water Tower Mall in Michigan Avenue, Chicago

- personnel, the type of people representing the company at all levels, especially at the retail outlets
- good management of costs and expenses: the chocolate confectionery industry is not uniformly labour intensive, but this company was, and raw material costs are not unimportant

Or again here is the president of a company that makes protective industrial clothing; the customers are typically other companies offering clients a variety of cleaning and maintenance services. The president identifies the KSFs as:

servicing customers' needs in a *timely* way; customers cannot carry very much stock, we get the order when the customer gets the order (i.e. typically a cleaning contract); one rental contract = 11 sets of garments – washed, wearing, and waiting

'execution quality' in the sense that the sets of garments have to be identical

OK, it is detail, but the detail counts and the company has been 'wound up' to get these details right and not some other details.

Here is the marketing vice-president of a company supplying gas to domestic and industrial users in the Deep South. It should be said straight away that this company faces a challenge in the sense that electricity is cheaper 'up front' – cheaper to install, equipment more readily available, shorter payback periods; the advantages of gas are middle term and the price differential *vis-à-vis* electricity has been erased. This executive responded to the author's question about KSFs by indicating:

customer service
quality service
price reduction with continuation of quality service

In developing the last of these points this executive noted:

The price of gas used to be much lower than that of electricity. Now the gap is closing. The TVA [Tennessee Valley Authority, an organisation set up in the New Deal period to dam the Tennessee river in the interests of flood control and hydro-electric power generation] have held electricity prices constant for four years, so we used to sell on price but now we sell on service.

To round off with, the insurance company CEO, whose reply to the question came back like machine-gun fire. KSFs are:

- premium growth
- return on equity
- general expense ratio (i.e. cost structure)
- mortality rate, i.e. premiums assume a particular mortality rate, but you need to keep measuring it
- lapse rates, i.e. controlling them
- yield rates on investments (they rose for years and then started to fall in the early 1990s)

Again readers may feel this is all 'taken for granted' stuff; surely higher managers all over the world can speak competently about key success factors for their companies. Not so in the author's experience, though again this is not a black and white contrast. Certainly one can ask about KSFs in discussions with European managers, but it needs to be done in a more gentle and less taken-for-granted way. The questioner needs to adopt a more conditional approach, ready for the possibility that the interlocutor may not have heard of KSFs and may need a quick, but appropriately low key, explanation; and then when the explanation has been offered you may be told it is all a load of high-falutin twaddle anyway. Also in Europe 'stopper answers' are not uncommon, where the manager says, rather gruffly, something like, 'Same as for any company – product, price, and service', which may be true but does not discriminate interestingly.

But the way Americans respond suggests they are not going through the motions to please you, this is not new to them, they have mentally rehearsed it a hundred times, and it is 'meat and drink' to them.

Key decisions

American managers show a similar readiness to identify and specify key decisions they have taken in the past. In my view it is part of the same phenomenon of conscious closeness to the operations – company – industry that goes with the development and articulation of strategy.

Here is our insurance chief executive again, reviewing the key decisions of his six years in the top position:

- developing a compensation agreement for agents
- repricing and redesigning of all products
- decision to consolidate operations in two states (following a merger); saved $40 million but made 500 people redundant

– re-engineering; 'looking at how we do business, at work flows, work processes and seeing what was *not* adding value. We mean to save $30 million all told, and will get to 15 million this year'

Or again the CEO of the mechanical engineering company whose strategic formulation was discussed in the first section of this chapter. Although the manager tended to understate his achievements he had in fact been brought in as a turn-round manager. His list of key decisions in office encompassed:

- putting *the* factory for one key product into a small town in rural Tennessee; i.e., green field site, away from the 'Deep North' and its labour relations problems, acquire younger labour force, and so on
- turning round the other key product: reversed decision to have it made in Korea
- pricing policy; charging different prices in different markets
- attaching importance to the sourcing (of raw materials and bought-out parts): 'try to focus on a few things and do them well'

Here is the vice-president of a company in the Midwest making a technically sophisticated consumer product:

> In the past the company that had been successful marketing via its 500 authorised dealers, decided to create a new division, selling outside the established distributors. 'This is an awful risk. It means we may undercut ourselves.'

> The company has committed a lot to TV advertising: 'it cost a fortune, but it paid off. We spent $10 million at one time! Part of it was to stimulate people to want the product, *and* to say [name of company] is my choice'.

> 'This is a borderless world', so set up subsidiaries in Japan and Spain; also set up a division in Germany, but it failed. 'But there is not much competition in Spain, and it is low cost.'

There is another theme running through these 'key decisions'. This is that they are quite bold, bolder than the European equivalent would be, with the buying and selling, moving of manufacturing facilities, bypassing of distribution systems, mergers, making people redundant, 'life-and-death decisions' about whether or not to manufacture in Asia.

Yet my main purpose with these examples is to show the readiness and the focus with which American executives responded to the question. Certainly one can ask the question of European managers, and one will get a lot of informative and revealing answers. But characteristically the answers will be more hesitant. And about every third interlocutor will tell you that management is not really like this, that there are not particular things that stand out (that the question is really in bad taste).

Yet we are citing this 'key decision consciousness' in the USA as part of a reflective involvement that is propitious for the development and explication of strategy. It is also one more manifestation of the individualism explored in the previous chapter.

Rhetoric or reality?

Finally in this consideration of strategic issues, if the starting point is the pronouncements of chief executives, it is only fair to raise the question of whether there is a gap between rhetoric and reality. That is to say, are the CEOs telling you things to impress you, saying what they think will sound good, or is it really happening? The question is particularly apposite given the bold nature of the changes and claims being made.

The scrupulous answer has to be that it is difficult to be sure without conducting a series of longitudinal case studies. At the same time there are reasons to believe that these executive claims match reality. One clue in this connection is their specificity. Those who would grandiosely mislead their listeners tend to deal in stirring generalities, yet many of the testimonies encountered in the study and selectively reproduced in the previous pages deal in specifics – this is where we put the new plant, this is the number of people we made redundant, this is how fast we provided service, and so on.

A second consideration here is that the testimonies refer to the past, typically to the recent past, rather than being expressions of questionable intent. And if one takes these two issues together – tangibility and recency – then they are in principle verifiable. Lastly, even as a 'one off' corporate visitor one was often shown the figures – turnover, market share analysis, profit movements, and so on. Indeed the American tendency to feel that the testimony was incomplete without the numbers was an additional point of interest.

5

Proactivity

The best way to predict the future is to write it.

Peter Drucker

So far we have offered a consistent picture. The first chapter touched on some of the proclivities and resources of American society. The next chapter focused these under the banner of individualism. The depiction of strategy that followed is a natural development from these premises of individualism, materialism, achievement. The present chapter takes a further step in the same direction by asserting that American managers, both singly and corporately, exhibit a consistently proactive strain. *Vis-à-vis* their European counterparts no black and white contrast is intended: again this is about a difference in degree, a difference of relative emphasis, but withal one that distinguishes the Americans.

What do we mean by proactivity? It is a mix of overlapping things, including:

– a starting conviction that humanity can shape the future
– that it is right to do so
– that 'points will be given' for trying, for the intention and resolve, rather than 'taken off' for failure; it is a matter of 'bare your chest' rather than 'cover your back'
– that targets for future achievement should be ambitious and demanding, rather than the reverse
– that we should anticipate future developments and get a grip of them
– that we are here to make things happen, not to 'mind the store'
– that the action that follows analysis is what is important, and the analysis is no more than a means to an end
– that in problem-solving the emphasis is on the solving, not on the introspective enjoyment of the problem

There is a further twist to it. Benjamin Franklin is credited with the *bon mot*: 'If a thing is worth doing, it is worth doing badly.' This little inversion of the English proverb is making an important point. This is that in the American scheme of things it is the proactivity to act, shape, decide, solve that is laudable; the actual programme, content, specifics are secondary. If these do not work one has lost nothing except time, and the right-thinking American will simply try something else, and keep trying until the objective is achieved. For Americans a solution that has a seven out of ten chance of success will be adopted; if it does not succeed something else will be tried, and something else again. And this 'if need be' serialised implementation of different means to the end is preferred to an eternal cogitation about the perfect answer.

The point can be made in a more down to earth way. Non-American observers of American companies often remark that Americans seem to chop and change: start something with zeal, give it up and go onto something else; indeed they seem to 'rack up' more than their share of failures, aborts and stall-starts. And the answer is yes, that is right, and it is because they attempt more, seek to achieve more, and at the end of the day want to be judged by ultimate achievement of ends, not perfectibility of means.

It is perhaps this disposition that is most striking. As one of my interviewees put it when asked about possible recurrent problems that he might confront in his role as CEO:

> I don't want to say that we have no problems but . . . when you have a problem, you look at it, stretch, grow; so it is not so bad to have problems.

Proactivity at large

Part of it is an endless setting of targets, and they tend to be ambitious targets, James Collins and Jerry Porras (1994) speak of better companies setting what the authors call 'big hairy audacious goals'. There was plenty of evidence of this in my study, and this applies to smaller companies as well as to the Fortune 500 set. Here is the sales-marketing vice president of a dairy in West Texas, asked about recent developments:

> We decided to get outside the 100-mile radius. Now we are hauling milk into a warehouse in Dallas. We bring back cartons, and the hauls lower transport costs.

Dallas must be a 5–6-hour drive away; it is a bit like an English dairy in say Reading deciding it was worth 'hauling into Newcastle'. Here is another example from Texas: a company that makes moulded plastic components for industrial customers. In 1986 the turnover was $4.5 million by 1992 it had reached $21 million and the company is still aiming to expand. The president, who has been in post since 1986, responds to a question about the most important things he has done since then by citing four key issues:

a decision to expand

a decision to change the organisational structure, from a rather un-differentiated model presided over by a general manager to a more functional structure

customer decisions, in the sense of:

- going for particular customers
- going for particular jobs

decisions about plant and buildings; part of the issue is that they have motor industry customers from Detroit and there is a need for them to be impressed when they visit

A nice positive mix here, with expansion and sales targeting, modernising the organisational structure and upgrading the plant and technology. Here is the CEO of the footwear company cited in the discussion of strategy. Here are his early decisions on taking over:

In the first two weeks I looked at sales by style number, and also at margins. There were a lot of lines with minimum sales and some low margins. So I gave the division heads a number – if you can't sell so many per annum then why not drop it if there isn't a good reason.

But if this cutting of the less profitable sounds a familiar story, note that these are negative acts with positive outcomes for the business:

I closed a couple of other labels. Plus a private division that was profitable – walked away from $0.7 million of business. But there was a 40% sales growth on a smaller range, a reduced asset base, and a better return on capital. I took a lot of people out especially in the first year. Also de-layered at general management level . . . Cut out a lot of fat, concentrated on the margins. Convinced people eventually.

Whatever the American business may be, it is not sentimental!

The essence of this proactivity is that it goes beyond operational need. It is not about 'minding the store' or keeping the plant ticking over. Instead it is about more, or better, or faster; about solving problems and removing road blocks.

The company that supplies gas to homes and companies has some difficulties *vis-à-vis* its rival electricity in that:

gas/gas appliances are dearer to install

they require more 'know-how' for their installation

a lot of dealers who sell gas appliances sell electric ones as well; left to their own devices they will tend to push the latter

One means the company has adopted to overcome this is to offer dealer programmes instructing dealers in the nature of the product and/or installation in the expectation that they will then recommend gas appliances to customers. The issue is discussed by the marketing vice-president and the domestic marketing manager. They agree to:

- go for a new dealer programme
- decide what things in particular dealers need to know (e.g. vent sizing, pipe sizing)
- decide to review their existing literature and videos and improve them if necessary
- reward the dealers for their participation in the programme by giving them free advertising of gas appliances
- confront the fact that the company's training department is currently overstretched so perhaps the programme should be mounted by marketing personnel (more push and more flair)

It is a low-profile, two-person exchange, but one aiming to advance the company cause with a set of neatly interlocked initiatives.

Meetings

The quality of proactivity explored in this chapter is typically evident in meetings in American companies. Decisions are taken, tasks are allocated, deadlines set. A European observer might think there was less analysis, certainly less fondness for it, than would be the case 'at home'; and perhaps less style, less wit, less humour, less subtlety, less deference, and less managed ambiguity. In the American meeting, rank and hierarchy differences will intrude less than in say France or Britain (though they are present). Power play will be more direct. Nothing that needs to be said will be unsaid for reasons of delicacy or interpersonal restraint. There are likely to be cross-checks on whether those present are understanding points being made. Someone who does not know something is less likely to (be allowed to) 'fudge it' (the semi-euphemism for 'I don't know' is 'I do not have that information').

But above all, American meetings move things on. At the end of an American meeting you know:

> what is going to be done
> who is going to be responsible for what actions
> when it is going to be done by

and the meeting may well break up when it has fixed a time for meeting again to review progress.

Problem-solving meetings are the American speciality. They are approached with prior conviction that all problems are solvable, and this is what we were put on earth for. The exposé of the problem tends to be a bit 'economical' by European standards, and the analysis (unless financial and/or quantitative) is rather more succinct than one is used to. There is also rather less claiming and disclaiming of responsibility for the problem, as though the view were, 'It does not matter where it came from, it is what we are going to do about it that counts.'

So the pattern is that the preliminaries are scaled down and the group will move quickly to the solutions and action. The solutions proposed are often not particularly elegant, original or resourceful; their *raison d'être* is rather that they worked 'someplace else' and look as if they have a chance of working here. The criterion is plausibility-practicability not perfectibility. If it does not work we will try something else. The strength shown on these occasions is:

– the decision *to do something*
– the speed with which the solution is generated
– the 'doability' of solutions

One of the many meetings I had the chance to sit in on was at a company that made high-quality shoes. The problem confronted was a quality failure on the part of a Mexican subcontractor. The meeting went through the issues of what they were going to do, who, how long, how much, and how the whole operation was to be controlled. Then the operations vice-president running the meeting 'signed off' the package with the remark: 'It may have some holes in it, it may work better than we think. It is a question of *getting in and trying.*'

Proactivity and advantage

Part of proactivity is angling for advantage, especially competitive advantage. Imagine you are running a hospital (in the pre-Clinton period). There are two key limitations to the amount of money you can make. One is that for ethical and social reasons the hospital may have to treat people who are uninsured or at least not fully insured, and make a loss on this or at least realise less profit thereon. But there is a silver lining! The insured and the uninsured do not have identical illness–treatment patterns. So one has to be strong in the specialisms dear to the commercially insured. Here is an East Coast hospital president on this theme:

> Obstetrics is a good paying area – paying women. Ditto cardiology, and it has grown substantially. So we grow the programme mix, and this leads to treating proportionally more fully insured people.

The second limitation on the profit capability of any given hospital is the fact that it is in competition with all the other hospitals in the area. And of course they compete in all the obvious, and perhaps some less obvious ways. Consider the role of technology. The case is put very neatly by our hospital president:

> Technology is an important device to build the level of quality. . . . technology costs large amounts of money; so if we spend $5 million on a piece of equipment, the smaller hospitals can't buy technology, so *we get their referrals*. We have found a blind hog!

(European readers might like an enlightening word on the notion of the 'blind hog'. A blind hog is a fat, juicy pig that everyone wants to catch and eat: and because it is blind, it will be caught – easily!)

To illustrate proactivity of a different *genre* one of the companies in our sample has a division devoted to inland water transport, by barge. In this connection it employs a lot of 'heavy' manual workers. At the time of their engagement these employees are given a very thorough medical. The primary purpose of this medical is to check any illness, deficiency, and above all disability that they may have *at the outset* of their employment, so that they cannot subsequently claim an occupationally induced disability and demand compensation for it. This kind of preventive rigour is typically American.

Or to take a more widespread example, consider drugs. Drug taking seems to be more widespread among ordinary American employees than among their European counterparts, or at least the employer 'response' suggests this. So drug-taking employees are a menace, drug testing is a counter-measure, and you test for drugs wherever and whenever you can. Several of the companies in our sample were in the process of acquiring other companies. At one of these the president held a series of meetings with immediate subordinates to discuss the take-over and how it could be managed. The following exchange ensued at one of these meetings:

> *Computer services manager*: Are we going to drug test?
> *Everyone present*: Yes!

The drug test is low cost, and it is important not to be had. So a simple questions evokes a chorus of assent.

Recourse to law

It is a commonplace that the USA is a litigious society. There are, indeed, more lawyers in the USA than there are farmers, and there are volumes of (anti) lawyer jokes. I would like to suggest that the recourse to law is yet another manifestation of American proactivity. Using the law is a way of getting your own way, getting something you want, stopping someone doing something to you, or just maintaining an 'on-guard' minatory stance – letting people know you won't be messed around lightly (like the Scots Guards).

To give one simple example: in the numerous cases among the companies I visited that were acquiring other companies, one of the things that was always checked out was pending lawsuits. You think about buying a company and so you ask: what lawsuits, who is suing them, and for what; and is the government proceeding against them, say for violations of the Equal Employment Opportunity (EEO) legislation, or are they being slammed for failing to comply with the Affirmative Action Programme (AAP) requirements?

Lawsuits just loom larger in the American consciousness, and that includes the managerial consciousness. And when you have none of your own to worry about you gossip about other people's. Overheard at the end of an American business meeting:

First manager: Have you heard about Wall-Mart being sued?
Second manager: No, what's the angle?
First manager: They are being sued by a repping company. Wall-Mart cut them out, and went direct to the manufacturer.

Proactivity predominates morality
The forces that drive proactivity sometimes take it beyond morality. In the earlier discussion of individualism we noted the tendency for success and achievement to be seen to legitimise whatever you did in their pursuit. These tendencies merge. Consider as a mild example the issue of manpower poaching; here is a case of the passive contemplation of sin, from the president of a technically sophisticated components supplier to big companies:

The problem is finding the technical people. For example a non-degreed process technician, he will earn more than a CPA [a qualified accountant]. And companies poach. *We would too if we knew where they were*; we just don't have the contacts.

Or a stronger example. On asking the hospital president about recurrent problems, he responded that 'every day' our doctors are talking to the competition (other hospitals that might like to have their services, reputation and power of referral). I queried the 'every day' bit of this formulation and was told that it was meant literally; on any given day at least one of the doctors would be having lunch with a rival hospital where at least some mutual 'sounding out' would occur. My next question was to ask how this could be countered, how would the hospital in question respond to the threat of losing to a rival a doctor they would like to keep? The reply was: 'You cannot always depend on their hypocrisy, but you can always depend on their greed.'

Proactivity and doing good in organised ways
The New World tends to differ from the old in that it believes in the perfectibility of human nature. This idea is not original, but still it might be worth spending a moment on the reasons for the difference. The New World takes a more optimistic view, a more life-affirming view, as the Germans would say:

- precisely because it is new; i.e., has had less (historic) time to find out it is wrong! (the cynical European view)
- because it has more land, space and resources, and therefore a greater capability to provide 'happy endings' for more people
- because an ethic of betterment was built into the motivation for coming to the New World in the first place

It is a short step from here to the proactive pursuit of improvement. Since something better is not only conceivable but realisable then why not 'go for it'? And do so in an organised way, with programmes involving a public statement of intent, the commitment of resources, the specification of means to achieve the desired end, and so forth.

This is the American, and particularly the American government's, way of getting things done. It has two consequences for business. First, the American government will launch such initiatives backed by legislation and the state's power to reward and punish. Examples from the 1990s would include the desire for environmental protection and improvement, the right to do justice to people suffering from some disability (the Americans with Disabilities Act came into force in the summer of 1992), and above all the wish to promote equality – between races, sexes and ages – in working life. The second consequence is that better companies will not only comply with such injunctions but will (appear to) internalise them as well, take them on board as their own, strive for their realisation – whether out of human decency or a desire to be seen as professionally flawless is not always clear.

In one of the companies I visited, privately owned but substantial, there was a strong commitment to gender equality and thus to the prevention of any form of sexual harassment. This was clearly inspired by the will of the owners, but as far as an outsider could judge, was accepted and applauded within the company. One simple manifestation is that the company provided a toll-free 1–800 number via which employees could report in confidence any presumptive instance of sexual harassment. What is more, this 1–800 number was in fact a line to the president's wife. Any reader who feels there is nothing remarkable about this should ask themselves if they can imagine such an arrangement in say France or England, or even for that matter in Sweden or the Netherlands.

In another of the companies, a substantial multinational, again in private hands, the owners had a deep commitment to environmentalism. In consequence practices in the company went far beyond what the law required. But even more striking is the fact that this company engaged in *initiatives* for environmental protection and improvement.

If we come down to a more tangible level companies will often 'proact' with regard to the government's programmes, making their demonstrable enforcement a priority. As an illustration, here (as always) is one of the companies in the study, in the Deep South, in the process of acquiring a smaller company in Maryland. The MHR vice-president and one of his deputies are discussing some of the implications of this:

> *Deputy*: It is heads up, let's be smart and not be caught by this. Let's find out if they do have an AAP [Affirmative Action Programme – i.e. can they demonstrate a real effort to hire minorities?]
>
> *MHR-VP*: Shall we call them straight away?
>
> *Deputy*: Fine

The ensuing telephone dialogue is only a one-sided demonstration of American proactivity, but it is such a gem it deserves to be quoted.

> *MHR-VP*: Do you have an AAP?
>
> *Local manager*: No
>
> *MHR-VP*: Do you like American roulette up there?
>
> *Local manager*: [*No reply, but sounds suggestive of annoyed resentment are audible over the wires*]
>
> *MHR-VP*: Do you track applicants, promotions, formations?
>
> *Local manager*: Yes
>
> *MHR-VP*: Is it in the right form for an AAP audit?
>
> *Local manager*: I don't know.

The MHR-VP then asks the manager in the Maryland company what she would have done if the OFCCP (the authority that monitors AAP) had visited. She replies: we would have called our lawyers!

Forget, for a moment, the fact that proactivity is not always reciprocal, and note the mind set of the initiators, which goes like this:

> check on it soonest
> are they doing it?
> can they show they are doing it?
> can they get it past the controlling authority?

Note also how 'straight' it all is: there is no nuance, no subterfuge, no English-style cultivation of acceptable appearance, just a straightforward getting on with it.

The natural gas company offers further examples, when managers proact to meet the demands of state governments. The state of Illinois, for instance, wants the company to do macro-economic modelling to show gains to customers of adding gas provision, and to include measures to make customers use less, that is, to be economical in energy consumption in the longer term.

Or consider Iowa. This was the first state in the territory of our gas company to go for demand management (the planned limitation of consumer demand). Iowa requires:

- the control of emission
- that trees be planted to match the energy burned
- that the state be treated as economically autarkic, such that no additional energy be 'imported' over the state line

Iowa has had rather a 'bad press' in American fiction: this is the state to which the luckless Captain Queeg of *Caine Mutiny* fame was banished. But in the matter of energy conservation it has sufficient clout for a gas supplier company two thousand miles away to be counting the cost of buying trees!

6

Systems

'It's as loose as a goose. It runs like Disneyland out of control.
They take decisions off the tops of their heads'.

American manager, just returned from a visit
to a company they are about to acquire

Like most non-Americans I got my first idea about what might be
distinctively American in business and management from contact
with American subsidiaries in Europe, in my case in Britain and
West Germany. These companies seemed to have a higher profile, to
proclaim their corporate identity and their Americanness. Their
managers were more assertive, more professionally aware, somehow
seemed to exude the notion that they were 'there to win' both
corporately and individually. And all this seemed to be reinforced by
higher remuneration, and more in-company mobility and promotion.

People coming new to these American subsidiaries were always
impressed in the first instance. They had a sense of having joined the
big league. There was a 'can-do' culture, a 'go for it' inclination.
The Americans don't mess around, they would say. Decisions get
taken, things get moved on. And especially in post-war Europe,
these companies seemed to be resource-rich. Whatever you needed,
you could have it. Resources would be hurled at problems, road
blocks blasted out of the way. The thousand-bomber raid was the
American art form.

Then there was something else that seemed to be different when
one had dealings with American subsidiaries in Europe. The people
who worked there, not Americans for the most part, seemed to be
better at answering questions. So if you asked, for instance:

what is your market share?
how do you decide how much to pay scientists in R & D?
is it cheaper to make it or buy it?
how do you recruit graduate trainees?
how is the budget monitored?

you tended to get pretty good answers – informed, clear, decisive.
You could see that somebody some time had thought it all through,
decided, and laid it out in stages others could follow. They never

seemed to 'fly by the seat of their pants'; instead they answered from a prepared position, and often one they seemed to have normatively internalised as well as understood. What one is observing here is the power of American systems.

Research on US subsidiaries in Britain

While my thoughts on American systems developed incrementally and as a result of a lot of separate company contacts and encounters a Scottish academic, Ian Jamieson, got there all in one go. Jamieson's doctoral research was on American companies operating in the UK, and the general question he addressed was: are they different from the run of indigenous British companies, and if so, in what ways? Jamieson wrote a book based on his PhD (Jamieson, 1980) and a few years later produced a neat summary of the findings (Jamieson, 1985).

Jamieson makes a number of contrasts between the American subsidiaries and the native British companies (and he also dismisses a few misconceptions) but central to his characterisation is the matter of what he calls formalisation (and we call system).

In Jamieson's view these American subsidiaries are distinguished by their high degree of formalisation (not formality), which means these companies tend to elaborate systematic procedures for dealing with contingencies. For example, Jamieson argues, their financial planning and budgetary control are more systematic, in the sense of being 'laid out', generally understood, covered by a set of procedures that are known, accepted, and comprehensible.

Or consider personnel, an area which in Jamieson's view lends itself admirably to American-style formalisation. In particular Jamieson suggests that personnel administration in the subsidiaries of American companies typically embodies:

- formal selection procedures
- written job descriptions
- person descriptions, in the sense of the characteristics of the person sought (*not* a philosophy of 'we'll know the right chap when we actually see him')
- recognised interview programmes
- management development programmes (rather than a traditional British *laissez-faire* stance to the effect that 'the right sort of person will rise naturally')

Or take marketing as another example. Jamieson argues that American companies will be better at assessing (new) markets: they will do this with more rigour, their assessment will be more systematic, and data-based; it will depend less on intuition, 'gut feel', and on what powerful people in the organisation think (the British style). Marketing campaigns among the American subsidiaries would be better planned, more detailed, would involve more specification (and monitoring) of objectives. Or again the Americans would sell their goods in more proactive and organised ways. They would not start until they were ready, they would have worked through the contingencies (and imponderables) and have plans to deal with them.

Now these ideas about formalisation (systems) are not all that Jamieson says but they are central to his theme. And his research-based testimony is particularly powerful when one remembers that he is talking about *overseas subsidiaries* of American companies in Britain – and if ever there was a culture that might have been expected to dilute and dissipate American energy and systems it is the British. Yet these American companies had managed to retain their proactivity and to reconstitute their systems on the other side of the Atlantic, and to do this through the medium of British managers and employees. This is a considerable tribute to their forceful professionalism and powers of cultural imposition.

Americans at home and the celebration of the system

In the time I spent in companies in the USA the celebration of the system was a leitmotiv. When interviewed, managers explained things to me, or when they dialogued among themselves, there were frequent references to the systems in place, and by implication to their intrinsic worth. The idea is caught by the manager quoted at the head of this chapter concerning the hopelessness of the company his organisation was about to buy. Loose as a goose, no control systems, no basis for rational decision-taking. Systemlessness is the ultimate American folly.

A variation on the theme is caught by our marketing vice-president at the natural gas company who remarked:

> If the numbers are close the intangibles may sway it; but if the numbers are wide, no we don't. And you have to watch people don't make the numbers what they need to be to fix the deal, to get approval, make it stick.

Is this not a neat encapsulation, where the numbers stand proxy for the system, and they come first, and the qualitative and intangible are allowed to fill any residual gap. Or the president of an injection-moulding company in Arkansas, a specialist component supplier for larger companies, responding to my question as to how his time is spent in a typical day:

> I get two or three calls a day from customers who have not had satisfaction from the usual channels. *First I check the systems are working.*

The emphasis here is unmistakable. Systems are there to make things work right. If things are not working right, then some system failure is the most likely explanation – and the first means of redress.

Roger Stone, CEO of Stone Container Corporation, addressing the annual conference of the Strategic Management Society in Chicago in 1993, spoke of his plans for the 1990s. The operations would be fact-based. There would be measures of performance. Indeed one of the missions was the establishment of a new long-term measurement programme. As Stone pithily observed: 'What gets measured, gets done.'

Later in his talk Stone confronted the problem of organisational change, and of selling change to tradition-centred company members – like older foremen. The company introduced a new quality programme, but without taking everyone with them. Stone formulated the problem in this quote:

> What do you do with someone who doesn't buy into the programme but does make his numbers? You fire him!

The ethic could not be clearer. Achieving production targets is not enough. You will have to 'do things right' and this means operating the current programme (system). And if not, . . .

The substance of systems

In the companies I had the chance to visit in the USA there was abundant indication that Jamieson had got it right. Any activity that could be planned, sequenced and put within procedural 'tramlines' was treated in this way. In a discussion with an MHR manager in the city transport authority, for example, I asked how they picked bus drivers.

It will start with any potential applicant for any kind of a job sending in a resumé (CV in English). And these are "entered into the system so that we can track them", whether or not there is any need for new employees at that time. They are sorted by specialism of course, plus a general employment category for cleaners. When a need for 'new hires' in a particular employment category arises there will be a random computer assisted pick which will generate a list of potential employees. In the case of bus drivers they will have to be over 21, and have a licence, and only individuals who satisfy these criteria will be picked by the computer. Those on the computer list are sent an application form. Then there is an investigation that:

> looks at their driving record from the state
> does a police check
> and employment verification: i.e. have they actually had the jobs they say they have had, and did they really leave for the reasons given on the application form?

'We lose some at this stage,' observed the MHR manager. 'Applicants have the opportunity to confess; if they don't we find out . . .'

The next stage is interview *and testing*, with the tests being job specific. For bus operators this will be:

> reading
> listening
> comprehension
> hearing
> simple maths

Plus a personal skills inventory, including a test of honesty. What is more there are tests that impinge on safety, and the propensity to commit theft and engage in violence. These tests are all multiple choice, and computerised.

Now the point is not that any of this is wonderfully original, but rather that Americans choose to do it in this way. There is no reason why bus drivers should not be selected in this way in say Poland or Portugal, but it probably does not happen, nor for that matter in England or France.

After the hiring comes the training, but let us consider as an alternative example the training operation in a restaurant chain. This is a nice example that raises a new challenge. This is, one is told, that many of the employees are illiterate. In a discussion with the MHR vice-president I query this, and the judgement is meant quite literally: there are people who cannot read or write. It occurs to me that I have never (knowingly) met an illiterate person, and mention this, which evokes the reply: 'Welcome to America!'

It also becomes clear that these illiterates are not Hispanic immigrants for whom English is a second language, but native born Americans who are victims of what this manager calls: 'the breakdown of the school system'. There is, furthermore, a strong suggestion that some bright and enterprising people are among the ranks of the illiterates. The manager speaks indeed of helping store *managers* to overcome the disadvantage of illiteracy.

The problem of illiteracy is compounded by that of turnover. High labour turnover is a feature of the catering industry, and in the case of this restaurant chain turnover ran at 200–300 per cent a year. Indeed some employees only stay 6–8 weeks.

But this is not bad news. This is a challenge to American organisation. Because of the poor quality of recruits, training is everything. This in turn raises the standing of the MHR function, where the training staff actually produce the training schedules and write the operating procedures. The MHR vice-president defines the training as:

nice and simple
broken down into easy steps (*voilà, l'esprit américain*)
using videos (bypassing the problem of illiteracy)
and using pictures; there are actually pictures that tell trainees 'when the hamburger is this colour, you take it out of the grill'

This example has not been explored with any muck-raking intention. Quite the reverse. Anyone can do things with college graduates, but it takes American know-how to run a smart operation with a bunch of illiterates who keep on leaving.

During the field work in the USA I had the chance to visit a bank and talk to a branch manager, which opened up the possibility of a comparison with branch banking in Britain. Now these operations in the two countries have more in common than in contrast: in both cases there is a high level of division of labour, specification of targets and quotas, performance measuring and monitoring. There were, however, some additional American touches of what Jamieson would call formalisation. The division of labour was higher, more functions in the American case were taken out of the branches and vested in regional and national headquarters. The targets and quotas were tighter, on a shorter time scale, and subject to more revision (from above). When I asked the manager about the areas of discretion that went with the job her reply was: 'A lot is decided for me', and she went on to say that she might take an overall target and break it down, assigning sub-goals to a variety of individual subordinates.

A British banker will always tell you that although rules and procedures are important there is a human element too – that interpersonal judgement, interaction, experience, 'feel' all have a part to play in deciding what to give to whom, and particularly in money lending decisions. This emphasis seemed relatively absent in the USA. Take lending. In America you cannot turn anyone down for a loan because you don't like the look of them, or for any reason that might be construed as discriminatory, such as:

sex
age
race
religion

Nor can a loan applicant in America be turned down for a loan because they are on welfare (social security); you can only turn them down on the basis of an income–repayment ratio. If the lending manager has reservations she or he can grant the loan but put the account 'on watch'; but if they do this they have to inform the customer and tell them why.

It is the same with opening a bank account. To do this you need:

$100 to open it with
two pieces of ID
a verifiable address
verifiable employment

There is also a national bad cheque reporting system. If you pass these tests, you cannot be refused.

In Britain, to fill out the comparison, to open a bank account one fills in a decorously vague form which does not ask you about your personal banking history, though you may have 'screwed up' at three other banks already and walked away owing each of them anything up to £2,000.

To take another dimension, anything relating to costs or costing that can be formalised and systematised will be so treated. In discussion with works managers in American manufacturing companies it is noticeable that they typically have a tight grip of costing, and can quote costs off the cuff. There are also typically systems that enable cost-calculations for non-routine operations based on 'standard hours' with labour, materials and overheads built in. Nor is this penchant for systematising costing restricted to manufacturing operations. Our hospital president explained his organisation's relationship to Medicare:

> Now Medicare pays up on a diagnostic related costing (DRC), that is, average predicted costs for treatments. There are 492 of them. The DRC includes the projected length of stay as well as the fee. These are not absolute; that is to say, you get a bit more if you exceed the norms. Blue Cross has also gone to DRC.

Personal remuneration is also invariably systematised. Here is the system at a religious-charitable organisation, an example picked on the grounds that it might be expected not to conform to the canons of professional rigour in such matters. This is how it goes:

1. Each employee fills up a form on the content and demands of the job.
2. The employee is assisted in this by his or her supervisor.
3. The form then goes to the remuneration manager, who evaluates the job in terms of:
   - know-how
   - problem-solving
   - accountability.
4. The remuneration manager's recommendation is then checked by a compensation committee (the point of the committee is not democratic appeal but standardisation/comparability).
5. The resulting individual pay is modified by periodic performance evaluations.

Now I am not suggesting that one would not find this kind of rigour and system in employing organisations in Britain (though not as much or as often), but where British companies do have a system like this it will probably be because it was devised for them by *American* consultants, most likely by Hay MSL.

Another twist to the American scene is that the systematising will often extend to areas which in, say, Britain are left to some amalgam of choice, trust and tradition. Take publishing. An American publishing house will have a permissions section. With regard to commissioned book manuscripts produced by its authors, this section will:

check references
check that permission has been given by copyright owners for any material introduced/quoted by authors
check that all quotes are acknowledged
check against plagiarism

In Britain this often is left to the author, in which case there is no real check as to whether or not authors do it (and the consequences of not bothering are usually nil). I mentioned this once to an American publishing executive who was showing me around the head office premises and he was deeply shocked: it confirmed his worst fears that life in Europe is nasty, brutish, and above all unregulated.

Causes and consequences

The system phenomenon which I have described and exemplified in this chapter probably owes its origin, like American efficiency in general, to the dynamic earlier in the society's history of few people and lots of space. The system is one way of economising with manpower, and getting uniformity of operation and outcome across space and distance.

I would like to suggest as well that the *penchant* for systems also sustains American egalitarianism. Systems standardise, in a sense it is their purpose, and by so doing they minimise differences between people who are affected by them.

Again, systematising activities and operations renders them more rather than less accessible. Systematising takes out the arcane, the idiosyncratic, the intuitive, and the bit that only gifted or clever people could do. Systems are anti-elitist. You want to paint the roof of the Sistine Chapel? Fine, you don't need Michelangelo, you need a system, and that way it won't take seven years.

The American discovery of the system also impacts on the craft ideal. It is often noted that America does not venerate the craftsman or the tradition of craft expertise in the way that Europe does, and this is usually ascribed to the relative shortness of American history – no Middle Ages, no craft guilds, and so on. As an alternative we would like to suggest that the craft ideal was displaced in the American case by discovery of the system, an alternative that enables 'ordinary people' to obtain efficiencies and results with larger numbers.

Furthermore the American love of systems has also affected attitudes to training. So that in the American scheme of things training is not so much in the specifics of knowledge and skill as in systems of operational handling. This is not, of course, a black and white contrast, but a question of relative emphasis.

As suggested in the first chapter, the liking for systems and the liking for information go together. In management the systems tend to be fuelled by information, with system responses being triggered by information inputs. Taking this a stage further the combination of systems and information in American organisations leads sometimes to a programming of decisions, where the manager takes a decision, but only when 'prompted' by the system.

American managers are generally perceived as being decisive by their European counterparts, as being more obviously and consistently decisive than is normal on the other side of the Atlantic. There are several reasons for this, most of which have been hinted at already. The American company typically has fewer constituencies to appeal to, fewer interests to square than its European counterpart locked into expectations of social responsibility and political control. The strongly developed sense of individuality, the norm of pro-activity, the general acceptance of the strategy imperative that have been explored in previous chapters are clearly all conducive to this decisiveness. And so, I would like to add, is a relatively high degree of formalisation, of dependence on systems and procedures, since they in a sense tell you what to do or at least trigger decisions. As the manager in charge of the bank branch said, 'A lot is decided for me.'

Finally the formalisation is a force for homogeneity. The systems are there for a reason. They encapsulate accuracy, uniformity, efficiency and cost savings. They help to get things done, economically. The systems are the essence of American professionalism in management. At the same time they leave less room for the individual, idiosyncratic and personal.

Foreigners (non-Americans) sense this. They are more likely to perceive a distinctly American style of management, to label some behaviours as 'typically American', than they are to perceive a typically French style or a typically Swedish one.

A Canadian commentator once described American managers as a flock of aggressive sheep. It is a good line, although unfair and unkind. Yet there is a strand of truth in this, when a proactive and strongly motivated group aggressively pursue the same objectives in the same way. Without the formalisation that has been the subject of this chapter that sameness would be rather less likely.

7

Free Speech and Self-interest

There's no such thing as a
shy American.

Canadian folk saying

In this chapter I would like to explore two themes; they are not
exactly related yet they overlap. The themes are general communication, and the articulation of both individual and corporate
self-interest. Let us begin with the communication.

Americans as communicators

The general view is probably that Americans are strong communicators. Or at least that they have strengths as communicators. That
is to say they are direct, and explicit, and their communicating is
often embellished by a certain forcefulness. This popular view is on
the whole confirmed by my study – and more besides. Let us take
first the issue of directness.

American English is typically more direct than British English,
and it is worth speculating about the reasons for this. There are
probably a number of factors. First, stronger individualism means a
stronger drive to communicate, with communication as the means
whereby the individual imposes on the human environment. Second,
the more uncomplicated way in which connections between means
and ends are conceived, a theme explored in the first chapter,
induces a more direct and forceful communication. There is less
need to temporise, to qualify, and to flag up ambiguities, to cover
the discourse in a little bit of irony. After all, if X leads to Y, and it
sure does in the American mind, then direct communication will be
part of the natural order of things, the activation of Y by X. Third,
the relative absence of class differentiation means that a certain set
of barriers is absent, those that concern the editing of communi-
cations between members of different social classes. It is not that
objective differences do not exist in the USA. Differences in power,
wealth, educational level and occupational status exist in the USA
as elsewhere – indeed some of these differences, for example wealth,
are more pronounced than they would be in most North-West

European states. But it is the subjective perception that has to be emphasised in the American context. The belief in classlessness is widespread, the attachment to equality is strong, the conviction that anyone can achieve and that the kid from 'the wrong side of the tracks' can become President is widespread. This subjective class-lessness is potent, and facilitates a common communication. A fourth and related point is that in American society achievement predominates over ascription. That is, what you do is more important than what you are; becoming is more important than being. As we have seen in the discussion of individual careers in Chapter 2, successful executives are likely to emphasise their variable origins in order to underline the magnitude of their achievement, whereas the British tendency would be to subtly suggest that the status one has now had always been enjoyed. This again is a proactive stance, and communication, direct communi-cation, is the handmaiden of proactivity. And finally Americans, especially Americans in organisations, are neither squeamish nor sentimental. In communicating they are unlikely to be restrained by considerations of refinement, social acceptability or image preser-vation. Anything that needs to be said is unlikely to be left unsaid for reasons of circumspection – again in contrast to many of their European counterparts.

Make it clear

This directness, this spirit of let's get it out in the open and make sense of it, was easy to observe in the study. For example when making a telephone call the initiator would come quickly to the point, even if the point happens to be one that a European might approach in a gentle way. Here is an executive from an air frame manufacturer who has just received a letter from a leading in-state university requesting sponsorship for an air cargo exhibition. His first words are: 'What kind of dollars are you talking about?' He gets an answer, and immediately asks: 'Obviously you have written to other people, haven't you?'

That is it: how much and how many. There is no hiding behind ambiguity here. Another company, where the MHR-VP questions one of his subordinates, June, on how a new internee (trainee) is doing. June offered a slightly vague answer, ending with: 'but I am trying to keep my nose above water'.

> *MHR-VP*: You mean you don't know?
> *June*: Yes, but it is not his fault

The same interlocutors: the discussion has now switched to man-agement personnel changes:

MHR-VP: I am glad you survived the transition.
June: I am glad you survived it too, because they vented all their irritation on you!

A different company, a shoe manufacturer, and the production manager is checking anticipated output with a management trainee:

Production manager: How many are you going to give me today?
Trainee: [*Proffers a rambling answer*]
Production manager: Now we've been through that, how many are you going to give me today?

The air frame manufacturer again, and the MHR-VP is being briefed by a group of subordinates so that he can handle better the upcoming negotiation with the labour union. He tells the group that his opener with the union regarding their benefits package will be:

- this is what you've got
- this is what it cost
- this is what it will cost with inflation
- this is what you will have to pay to keep it the same

'How's that sound as an opening salvo?' he asks his subordinates (and the answer has to be, 'All right' as long as they are American). Next he tells the group: 'You need to tell me where I need to end up; we'll talk about strategy later.' In other words establish the objective first, then we know what we are shooting for, then we will work out how to achieve it.

Judgements on individuals, and on what to do with them, often have the same sharpness. In this company the president and the controller are discussing the fate of the managers at an about to be acquired company:

Controller: What about Al? [the controller at the about to be acquired company]
President: He's a hack, he's not anyone you need.

The controller accepts Al's limitations, but argues that perhaps they need to keep him on for 30 days to close the books. Then she queries the remuneration package with her boss.

Controller: But we don't need to put him on benefits?
President: No, just a flat rate as a consultant.

Another company, and another acquisition:

Computer manager: Now people issues. Shall I be axing the guys I don't need?
CEO: No, only two of them, and put them on a three-day contract

Another feature of American dialogue is closure. It tends to be explicit, you know when you have come to the end. Here is the shoe manufacturer again, and the manufacturing vice-president has been chairing a trouble-shooting meeting on a quality problem.

Manufacturing VP: What else do we need to discuss?
Production manager: That should do it.

This terse reply is American for: we don't want any damn fool raising irrelevancies under Any Other Business just because they like the sound of their own voice, so let's get the hell out of here and start making it happen.

Making sure

Another feature of American interaction is the pervasive desire to check. There is an endless desire to check that people have understood, that they know what they need to know, that they get briefed, that all parties to an operation have the right information. In the first few minutes of sitting in on the work of an American manager I heard:

does she realise there will be changes?
have the pay section been told?
do you want to come for a briefing?
do you understand this?

One has to make sure messages have been understood. Here an MHR vice-president and one of his subordinates are discussing calculations on an employee Medicare scheme:

MHR-VP: Do you understand what I am asking?
Colleague: I am going to multiply this figure by this, and divide by this.

A different company but the same subject, costing alternative medical benefit programmes and their constituent parts. The MHR vice-president is working it through with his colleagues:

MHR-VP: What does that mean?
[*They tell him*]
MHR-VP: Is that a reasonable request?
[*They give him a judgement*]
MHR-VP: OK, great, I understand that

The same meeting, and the chairman checks that Bill, one of those present, knows what it is all about:

VP: Bill, are you following what we have been talking about?

It does not look as though he is, and Pauline is called upon to give him a run-down.

Pauline: Does that make sense?
VP: No.

More explanations, then a contribution from Bill.

Bill: Do you get my point?
Pauline: Yes I get it. How do I stop that?

Another company, this time a discussion of hiring and firing tactics following a take-over. At the end of the discussion the president asks one of his subordinates: 'Are you clear what you gotta do?'

It is the archetypal American question at the end of the discussion of any issue.

Hierarchy without deference

Newcomers to American organisations are sometimes misled by the equality of manners, outspokenness and ethic of approachability into believing that the hierarchy has no teeth. Not so. American managers will use authority with less circumspection than many of their European counterparts. The American view of power is simple – it is a resource, and you use it. You use it to advance the business, move things forward, remove road blocks and to crush the opposition. Anyone who bucks the system, who opposes in the wrong place, at the wrong time, in the wrong way, who goes too far, is going to get busted more surely and more speedily than their European counterparts. The quip that America is 'The easiest place in the world to get a job. And the easiest place to lose one' is typically cited by Europeans who mean to play up the first part since they are impressed by the USA as a society where it is possible to get in, get on and get up like no other. But the second part is equally cogent. For anyone who opposes in an American organisation less time and effort is likely to be invested in:

    patching it up
    saving face
    finding a compromise
    winning over the deviant by argument and persuasion

After all this is a proactive society where things get done, and it is easier to simply neutralise the opposition.

Notwithstanding all this, indeed surprisingly in the light of these considerations, America remains a non-deferential society. This shows in the communication patterns of those who work in its corporations.

To take a simple manifestation, American secretaries are rather less deferential than their counterparts in many European countries. They typically give every appearance of efficiency, will be strong on initiative, and will not be shy about taking decisions in place of or in support of their bosses, but they do not render much deference They are often quite brusque in their speech. They say things like 'I'm going to lunch now', where the British version would say something like: 'I'm off to lunch now, if that is OK' or 'If you don't need me I'll go to lunch now.'

In the same spirit they announce intentions to take time off, to do things when it is viable for them, to pass on assignments to someone else if they figure they are too busy or that the assignment does not warrant their personal attention.

Receptionists/switchboard operators in American companies are a variation on the same theme. The idea that one ought to be cringingly polite to any caller in case they happen to be the Queen or the President does not commend itself. The responses on the telephone are more brisk (and brusque), matter of fact, and sometimes even tart. Yet at the same time, American switchboard operators are more helpful. They deal with inquiries not in terms of deference and status, but in terms of function and need. When you are waiting in the reception area of American companies you hear little snatches of telephone dialogue like:

> You want Sandra in marketing!
> We got four Sandras.
> You tell me what it's about.
> I'll get you the right one.

> You want Purchasing?
> We got 300 people down there.
> What you selling? I'll find you the person to talk to.

It is very much the same among managers. In their interactions with superiors they will typically:

- ask them questions back (rather than mutely accept an order and go away and wait for inspiration as to its meaning)
- tell them when things ought to get done, i.e. remind their bosses of *their* obligations
- occasionally redefine contributions: e.g. 'I'll get Carol to do it' equals I am not going to do it myself
- announce their own plans, like 'I am taking this afternoon off because my niece is in town, I'll do it tomorrow'

Here for example is the marketing vice-president of the gas company in discussion with one of his report-to's (as Americans like to describe immediate subordinates), Jane. They are discussing different ways of organising the training programme for the dealers who sell gas appliances – the way it has been done before, and the way she wants to do it. He is flexible, inclined to compromise:

> *Marketing VP*: Is some combination of these programmes the way we need to go?
> *Jane*: You've given me a whole new twist, and I need to think about it. [Note, not: 'It's a great idea, Sir' (and I will go away and try to quietly subvert it while doing what I want and maintaining a semblance of compliance).]

The conversation moves to the direction of who is 'a preferred dealer'; he is worried that they cannot, so to speak, 'quality control the status', that you might get some jackleg plumber so labelled alongside the more respectable dealers. Jane's response is: 'I have thought on this but I have not come up with an alternative yet.'

Note that there is no apology, no excuses being made. The message is sober yet matter of fact:

> Sure, it is my job to think about it. And I have. But I have not cracked it yet.

And there is a further suggestion that she will eventually crack it, and when she does it will be her version that will prevail – but he is vice-president!

A little later their discussion moves on to the question of how much they are charging for *replacement* water heaters. Too much, in Jane's view: 'This is almost like gouging our present customers.'

The cost turns out to be $400 plus and Jane is appalled: 'For our *present* customers, you explain that to me.'

The vice-president does. He runs the calculations, and is able to show Jane that the company only makes $53 on these installations. She is unimpressed, and unrepentant, and asks: 'How do our reps handle that?'

In other words, even if you can give me a good rational explanation, it is still wrong; the customers will resent it and it is bound to make difficulties for our sales people.

Here in another company is a discussion between the president and the purchasing manager about the operations of another company they are about to acquire. The issue is pricing policy. In this business, the distribution system is tiered. The about to be acquired company sells lower down the distribution chain than the acquiring company, and therefore at lower prices. This means there will be pricing inconsistencies after the take-over, and the purchasing manager is worried:

> *President*: I found I used to have your attitude and think there was no way a company could do it.

> *Purchasing manager*: I did not say no way! I said we should address it, and I am concerned.

Again note the mature tone of the response. It is saying:

> I am not going to defer to you because you are president
> I have a valid point of view
> And that is not to be simplified or misrepresented, so that you can 'see it off' on the basis of your experience

There is a certain paradox here. This is that Americans tend to be less deferential and more independent in the expression of their views, but in organisations where the power-holders above them are more likely to use that power if they feel it is necessary. It is a dangerous business being American, and not just in Gary, Indiana.

This tension is perhaps also reflected in American humour. In my experience there is rather less joking in American companies than in British ones, and certainly the diffuse humour that is part of any collectivity in Britain is largely absent (Barsoux, 1993). What joking does occur is more in the form of wisecracking, often annexed to an assertive individuality – where one makes cracks to push home one's point or to undermine the presentation made by rivals. When joking goes beyond this it often has a slightly war-weary, battlefield tinge to it, an acceptable acknowledgement of the strains of corporate life. As one of our executives put it in a telephone conversation with a colleague: 'You know, when you are ready to go out on stress, you need to transfer to California.'

Euphemism?

So far we have explored the positive elements in American speech – direct, outgoing, independent-minded and with start and closure. But it may be worth pausing for a moment to ask if there is a reverse side to the coin. Are there any indirect, oblique or euphemistic elements in American speech?

Although it does not fit the pattern or the image, I would like to suggest that there are, and indeed that such bits of indirectness are observable in talk in organisations. To take an obvious example, no American seems able to say 'I don't know', especially in response to an inquiry from a boss (or outsider). Preferred alternatives are:

> I do not have that information
> That data is not available to me

or better still one can shift the responsibility a little more with:

> I do not think we have that information at this point in time.

Note again the penchant for information rather than knowledge explored in the first chapter. The information emphasis also serves an excusing-depersonalising end. A lot easier to admit that no one has the quarterly sales figures for branches in Alabama than that you do not know about developments in corporate thinking.

It is also clear that there are more conditional, indirect ways of getting people to do things. Here is a vice president discussing with his second in command the production of some decision/programme that the president wants:

> *VP*: We need to accelerate this because it has been outstanding for so long.

VP goes on to ask if it can be done by phone. Second-in-command says he would rather do it in writing so that it is done in a more than perfunctory way.

> *VP*: Would it make sense to call them first, then follow it up with a memo – best of both worlds?

This little exchange is positively English!

The same executive, this time on the telephone to opposite number in an about to be acquired company where the initiator is chasing a report relevant to the take-over deal:

> *VP*: You are probably better organised than I am so it will happen real fast.
> *Opposite number*: Let's not have a race on this one.
> I'll send it down as soon as I can find it.

How is that for an oblique command, tempered by a conditional response?

The gas company again and their training programme for dealers. The marketing vice-president has a plan that will involve the company's sales force, but his interlocutor is not happy with this:

> It means taking commission reps off their work.
> I'd have some questions about that

This sounds to an outsider like 'over my dead body'.

The same company, and another manager is in discussion with the marketing VP. The issue this time is that the manager wants to buy more from one already major supplier to the company, at the expense of other suppliers (his motive is not really clear). His suggestion does not get a sympathetic response, and he signs off with the remark:

> I don't know how to draw the line on how much a company can eat to be loyal to a big cat.

Not exactly challenging, but it does suggest the possibility that the vice-president does not know either, and may be drawing it in the wrong place.

Or again, an MHR-VP after a composite briefing session with a group of his report-to's observes with manifest good humour:

> I'm going to have to ask you guys to follow up on all this stuff; I don't really have time to do that.

This, we can safely assume, is American for this is a whole heap of hassle and I am going to dump it on you!

Self-interest and the quality of speech

Probably the strongest conviction that non-Americans have about American speech is that it is zappy. It communicates action imperatives, it gets to the heart of the matter, it produces cynical and worldly judgements fast, and lays bare motives at the drop of a syllable. In doing the study it seemed to me that this quality of speech, sneakingly admired and often imitated by non-Americans, flourished particularly in expressions of self-interest, whether individual or corporate.

One of the companies in the study had recently acquired another substantial company at the other end of the country. This led to serious personnel work, a lot of things to be decided and administered. As an outsider one got the impression that the staff of the acquired company were all 'on the make', trying it on, alert to the possibility of grabbing some further little advantage for themselves. It gave rise to some interesting exchanges.

The acquired company is being integrated, with many of its operations moved to the sites of the acquirer and many of its staff transferred to the acquiring company's headquarters. One of the incoming managers is told on the phone that 'we need to discuss pre-existing on dental', i.e. they need to make sure this guy does not claim his teeth went wrong after the move and he rips them off $1,000. Another would be transferee who claims she cannot rent a comparable house in the new location and is forced to buy to maintain her status, and wants a special deal. A third manager has moved already, but she has encountered some pollution problem in connection with her new property and wants the company to pay for it, a claim dismissed by one of the MHR managers with the remark: 'She's just fishing'. Another of these resourceful claims against the acquiring company evokes the comment: 'I don't mind that, so long as she don't go too far'.

Another company, another acquisition, this time of a bankrupt company. The acquiring company has devised some scheme whereby they can acquire the company's assets and inventory but without *legal identity* (debts and obligations).

As the finalisation hour for the deal approaches the top management have endless discussions about how the various contingencies are to be handled. The purchasing manager, for instance, is worried about the bankrupt company's warehouse – it is leased, and it is too small. The president reassures him:

> Call the landlord when we open, renegotiate here, get a better deal, terminate if you want.

The purchasing manager looks unconvinced, and the president adds:

> You can deal because they're hung out to dry. They got a lease with a default company!

In another discussion it emerges that two of the workforce of the bankrupt company are labour union members:

> *President*: Ignore it.
> *Purchasing manager*: I'm not happy with this.

The controller volunteers that she won't deduct the union dues on the payroll, but the purchasing manager is still uneasy, fearing someone may come in and try to unionise.

> *President*: Talk to the people; do you want to work for us, we don't have a union.
> *Purchasing manager*: Is that legal?
> *President*: No

Next, to computer hardware which the bankrupt company has leased from IBM. The suggestion is made that they should contact IBM, and offer to take over the unexpired part of the lease for the computers – but at a reduced rate of course (apparently IBM have brought out a new model since the bankrupt company started the year's hire). But the computer services manager (CSM) sees a snag here:

> *CSM*: IBM have not been paid. If I alert them with a phone call maybe they send in a truck and get their machine on Sunday afternoon.
> *President*: We'll have the locks changed same day.

Computer software is another challenge. The bankrupt company leased its software. The software company have already agreed a deal with the new owners, and offered to come and give them a demonstration, on the premises of the bankrupt company, when the purchase of the company has been finalised. But there is another angle. The owner of the bankrupt company is suing the software house, claiming their defective software caused his company's bankruptcy – a nice American touch this (nobody believes it, of course). But G, the former owner, also claims that the software house 'put a "drop dead" code in, and then blackmailed us to pay to take it out'. Interestingly, everyone is prepared to give credence to this story. The computer services manager observes that the software house may indeed have 'put a crater or a bug in the system to block usage'. Everyone is happy with his suggestion that they should have the new user demonstration on the software house's own premises.

Another all-American issue. They are all agreed that the bankrupt company will sell anything and everything it has in stock (most of which it won't have paid for) in the final hours before the purchase deal goes through – what a nice way to raise a bit of money at the eleventh hour. So the buyers expect to take over a heavily de-stocked company. What is more, a lot of what the company will sell under its new owners has to be imported first, and this will take time, so how long will it be before this acquired company has anything to sell? The purchasing manager is worried, but the president is made of sterner stuff:

> *Purchasing manager*: That's scary
> *President*: Yeah, but it's all you've got, and you got to run with something.

Like a John Wayne movie isn't it?

8

Industrial Relations

Warum gibt es keinen Sozialismus
in den Vereinigten Staaten?

Werner Sombart

Werner Sombart's question – why is there no socialism in the United States? – is more often posed than answered. It is posed because it seems to open the door onto an American setting, where there is indeed no serious socialism, where certain phenomena are different and have to be accounted for in a different way. American trade unionism is like this.

A non-ideological unionism

It is because there is no socialism that trade-unionism is largely non-deological. Trade union membership does not indicate an anti-capitalist ideology, does not indicate an affiliation with a left wing political party, and says nothing about working class solidarity. Union membership is about the utilitarian and the calculative, tempered by the traditional and the geographic.

Depending on whose figures you believe, trade union membership rates are not high in the USA. Indeed they are less than half those of major industrial countries in Europe such as Britain and West Germany (it is better to stay with a comparison with West Germany as was; German re-unification in 1990 rendered union membership figures meaningless in the short term). Not only are American rates low, but they are also industry specific, or at least higher in a collection of mostly old-fashioned industries – steel, coal, trucking, autos, heavy engineering and so on. And again, and more markedly than in Europe, trade union membership is geographically specific as well. People join unions in the North and North-East, and in some places on the West Coast (like the port of Los Angeles). This geographic clustering is partly a reflection of the fact that these are areas of traditional manufacturing, but it also reflects industry and plant migration within the USA. This migration is typically from north to south and also to some extent from north-east to south-west. As one of the CEOs in the interview sample expressed it quite boldly: 'We came down from Ohio to Tennessee to get away from the UAW.'

In some cases the north to south migration is substantial to the point of revolutionary. Where is the centre of the American automobile industry, for example? And before plumping for Detroit just remember that within an hour's drive of Nashville, Tennessee there is the GM plant at the side of Interstate 65 near Bowling Green, Kentucky; and to the south of Nashville, on the same highway leading down to Alabama there are both the Nissan works and the showpiece Saturn works of GM, both within easy commuting distance of Nashville.

So unionism in the USA is restricted, non-ideological, not politically aligned, centred in traditional industries, and in certain parts of the country. Certain things follow from these premises.

Avoidable unionism

The most important is the employer and managerial conviction that unionism is avoidable, and on the whole this is right. Trade union membership is preventable in the USA in a way that it is not in 'old Europe' with its survivals of doctrinaire socialism, traditions of working class solidarity, and associations between unions and left wing political parties – the Labour Party in Britain, the Partij van de Arbeid in the Netherlands, the Social Democratic Party in Sweden, and so on. Because the traditional, sentient, ideological dimension is largely lacking in the USA, union membership can only be calculative and utilitarian – about gain, benefits, and to a lesser extent protection. And the American view is that if these things are on offer anyway – pay, conditions and benefits are good – there is no need for employees to join a union and for the most part they will not do so.

Again, various things follow from this. First, companies will have an explicitly anti-union orientation. Preventing the unionisation of the plant or company is likely to be an explicit 'war aim'. Second, companies are likely to 'tool up' to achieve this war aim. They will train first line supervisors and line managers in 'union avoidance', in handling and defusing grievances. Third they will, when times are good and companies have to compete for employees, put effort and creativity into the development of benefits, competitive benefits, benefits that are at least a bit better than those offered by the company down the road. Fourth, they will try to make the administration of both salary and benefits efficient, unlikely to give rise to employee irritation; an employee whose wages are short and who 'has to go down to the pay office to sort it out' is a potential defector to the union. Fifth, you actively discourage union member-ship by means of personal pressure, as we have seen in excerpts quoted in earlier chapters. One example of the (non-union) company response occurred during one of the interviews, when an on-site line manager at an outlying manufacturing location telephoned in to headquarters to report that a 'new-hire' was soliciting for union membership among his new workmates. The receiving vice-president's response was instinctive, and the line manager:

– was exhorted to inform the company president
– was advised on what law firms to consult
– and told to check the laws in Arizona to see if they could get the offender for soliciting during working hours

After the telephone conversation the vice-president observed that when something like this happens 'it is like the Israeli army mobilising'. Of the culprit in this story the headquarters executive dryly remarked: 'This guy is unlikely to have a long career with us!'

Simple moves rather than system

The phrase the 'system of industrial relations', beloved of under-graduate course designers and textbook writers in Britain, is singularly inappropriate in the USA. This phrase, with its conno-tations of rules, acknowledged procedures, parallel institutions, not to mention reciprocal expectations and industrial responses, is a far cry from the American scene of interest-driven pugnacity. In the USA there is no system, it is all more basic. If the company is non-union it will fight to keep it that way; anyone who wants to unionise it must be prepared for a fight. If the company is unionised it is an article of management faith that union power must be contained, that the management prerogative will be preserved at all costs, and that the company will be on the defensive at all times, ready to fight organised labour if it has to. The last point, the readiness of employers to resist the union and union pressure whenever needs must, is reflected in the taken for granted things managers say. One CEO, for example, asked innocently on our side if union contracts were annual, replied that annual contracts would be awful as the company would then: 'spend all its time laying in inventory against a strike'.

Fighting strikes

Strikes, of course, must always be fought. The employers' stock-in-trade here includes lock-outs, firing strikers, engaging 'new-lines', and above all management will take over and run the plant, as best they can, with the support of white collar workers and supervisors. And again since employees know that in the event of a strike managers will try to run the plant it makes sense to try to frustrate their efforts up front – by sabotage. Indeed in the run-up to the union contract negotiation a bit of sabotage is quite normal. In the old days it was impairing the machines and destroying the repair manuals, nowadays messing up the computer memories of equipment is the order of the day. And of course both sides will try to frighten each other. In one company I visited in the approach to the contract negotiations many employees sported T-shirts with a rattlesnake motif and the legend: WE DON'T WANT TO STRIKE BUT WE WILL IF WE HAVE TO.

In one of the companies visited a strike had occurred at the end of the 1980s, a classic American strike where unionised workers withdrew their labour and management ran the plant, in this case for more than two months. Although it was only the blue collar workers who went on strike, if the decision to carry on running the plant had not been taken the white collar workers would have to have been laid off: this meant it was not so difficult to 'recruit them' into temporary manufacturing roles. So the plant was run by a combine of managers, supervisors and clerical workers – many of them women. Some of these clerical workers went straight to jobs in manufacturing, others went on makeshift training programmes first.

There is a further twist to the story, and this is that the 'stand in' manufacturing workers made a video – about themselves running the plant during the strike. The reason for making the video was moral and psychological. Those involved did it to pep themselves up. This video, which was run for my benefit, emphasised the 'stand in' workers' attempts to perform the tasks of the regular manufacturing workers. The picture that emerged was three parts novelty appeal and one part heroic. The supervisors drove the product out of the door because the teamsters (lorry drivers) would not cross the picket line. The video showed highlights, such as one of the vice presidents serving lunch for the new workers. It also captured various high points in the struggle. A speech by the corporation president, for example, informing the new workers that the output and standards achieved were superior to those attained by the regular workforce. Another 'high point' was when the company decided to put its drinks machines around the works onto 'free vend'; it came over as rather like the decision of the British RAF (Royal Air Force) not to put any limit on the bar bills of fighter pilots during the 1940 Battle of Britain. Indeed the Second World War analogy was quite poignant throughout. The video had about i an aura of heroic amateurism enjoying its 'finest hour' in the face of epic adversity.

I have highlighted this video, even though it is a 'one off', because of its indicative power. They strike, we resist. By striking 'they' have used the ultimate deterrent. We, management, are perhaps not so well placed, but we have resources – of willpower and ingenuity. And when we, management, get started 'defending our corner' we will throw in everything we have got. And we sure have a better grasp of how to achieve motivational lift than they do.

Industrial democracy and the USA

It probably goes without saying that there is no industrial democracy, in the formal European sense, in the USA. Indeed expressions such as 'industrial democracy' and 'co-determination' are not actually meaningful in American English. To convey their substance one has to paraphrase and enlarge. And however nice a guy you are speaking to you will note a perplexed expression, a furrowing of the brow. In the South such deviations as worker democracy are in fact likely to be described as communism.

A further twist is that as far as one can see there is no actual demand for these things on the employee side either. The employee view is rather more along the lines that *more* – pay, benefits, or whatever – would be nice but why the hell would one want to share the managers' job with them, making decisions, being responsible? After all that is what they get paid for, and are we going to do this for them – without the rank and pay?

It is an interesting aside, but American companies have sometimes got into trouble in Continental Europe for violating the industrial democracy requirements. In countries with a formal system of industrial democracy, based in law, it is all too easy for the subsidiaries of US companies to find themselves in difficulties (Lawrence, 1991). One can almost hear them thinking, these requirements 'can't be for real'; worker representations on the board of directors, who is kidding who here? This polite incredulity may then be followed by the characteristic American resolution to preserve the management prerogative at all costs, and what do you have – a company that is in trouble for breaking the law.

It is not that Americans in general or American companies in particular are lawless. The law does weigh with them, but it is not an absolute. It is something they will take account of, but there are other considerations, and these might in fact outweigh. This orientation was expressed very nicely by one of the interviewees, a vice-president in a company with manufacturing subsidiaries in

Germany. These were circumscribed by German requirements concerning overtime working. In Germany some limits are placed on overtime, in part to preserve family life where some 'common time' has to be guaranteed, in part to prevent a situation where companies make line workers work longer as an alternative to engaging more workers. The practical consequence is that companies in Germany are only allowed to institute a limited amount of overtime working on their own initiative, and thereafter overtime intentions have to be communicated to the *Arbeitsamt* or labour office, which might withhold its permission. This was the situation with which our American vice-president was faced. His revealing comment was: 'If we break the law, we break the law. Our first duty is to our customers.'

The labour contract

In the mid-1990s these contrasts were typically triennial, negotiated every three years. The negotiations are at plant level, rather than company level. This in itself is revealing. The American (management) view would tend to be, why should we give them 5 per cent in Arkansas just because we had to in Pennsylvania?; and even more revealing, the employee view would tend to be, why should they get 5 per cent more in New Mexico just because we have had the muscle to wrest this from the employers in the state of Texas?

Furthermore, contracts cannot be negotiated at an industry level, where industry connotes a block of separate companies who happen to manufacture a similar range of goods. First of all, there is no machinery for such a negotiation as there is for example in Germany or even more in Sweden. Second, it would cut across, indeed expunge, the American individualism I highlighted in the second chapter, an individualism which is as strong at the level of the company as it is at the level of the single person.

So the contract negotiation is at plant level. And on the management side, in any reasonably sized company, it will be fronted by the most senior MHR person, rather than by the chief executive. And the negotiation of this contract is the single most important thing that the MHR-VP can do, the ultimate in executive macho. So how does it proceed?

The parties have to notify 60 days before the end of the old agreement that they want to renegotiate. The trade union comes in with its 'laundry list' and management comes in with a list of things that 'need to be changed'. The actual economic position of the company, and what it might be capable of paying, is only discussed in the last few days. If the wage claim is in fact rejected one may expect a 'works stoppage' (strike), though these days employees may continue to work and negotiate at the same time. Until a new agreement is in place, the old one is valid in law.

So what do the two sides ask for? On the union side it is typically wages, benefits and working conditions. There is no obvious priority in there. The unions are political, not in the sense of ideological allegiance, but rather because union leaders are selected and retained because they are politically popular. To sustain this popularity they have to 'win a few', but they do not want to have their hands tied before they go out to bat!

On the other side, the 1990s saw the emergence of a typical management agenda, which might include: measures leading to cost-saving and efficiency, often in the form of 'downsizing' with de-layering (taking out a given hierarchical level, say that of senior foreman) as an extra; building in greater workforce flexibility, especially as regards manufacturing tasks by changes in working conditions and practices, thought likely to lead to cost savings and greater flexibility; reductions of benefits granted earlier, with an emphasis on 'take aways'.

This is not, it has to be said, an especially happy state of affairs. But the times when unionised workers in traditional industries would ask employers for substantial rises which the company would then pass onto customers, without any short-term effect on their competitive position, have gone. We do not know if these days have gone for ever.

It may be helpful to point up the American reality by means of a comparison with Britain (Table 8.1). There are things that these two Anglo-Saxon countries have in common in matters of management and business life, and a tradition of adversarialism in industrial relations is one of them, albeit more pronounced and explicit in the case of the USA. To offer a sharper contrast with America we will also include a continental European country, Sweden, that has a long socialist tradition (Lawrence and Spybey, 1986).

Finally, in the following table we have, at the risk of over-simplifying, identified benefits as the key issue in American labour contract negotiations. This needs to be unpacked a little, and there has been some change over time.

First of all the American government has provided rather less in the way of welfare than has government in north-west European countries. This has left American citizens with a greater need for social security provision than their European counterparts. In part this need has been met by employee initiative in the form of individuals protecting themselves against misfortune by means of private insurance. But the need has also in a large part been met by

Table 8.1 *Comparative industrial relations*

	USA	UK	Sweden
Trade union membership rates	Low	Medium	High
Ideological basis to unionism	–	–/+	+
Class consciousness important for union membership	–	+	–/+
Union membership diffusely meaningful for individual	–	+	+
Union movement attached to political party	–	+	++
Level of bargaining	plant	variable	industry
Key issue in bargaining	benefits	wages	conditions
Management response to strikes	fight	sit out	Avoid/negotiate
Presumption of community of interest between management and workers	–	–	+
Attitude to industrial democracy	very negative	negative	positive

employers, who have 'deputised' for the state in providing social security cover and especially medical services for employees.

Second, during the golden age of American superiority after the Second World War benefits naturally expanded in range and developed in quality. In the scramble for manpower in a period of economic expansion benefits were a competitive weapon. Companies attracted and then retained employees because of the quality of the benefits they offered. Benefits administration had to be good (no 'foul ups') and companies also put creative energy into the development of benefits, packages and options. And even though the economic climate has changed, this is still in part true. Employers may still attain a competitive advantage *vis-à-vis* each other through benefits, by what in strategy terms would be termed niche or differentiation approaches.

Third, however, the economic climate has changed. The USA has lost the unique set of post-war advantages, Japan is an ascendant rival, and the EU is a bigger market. Furthermore, as Thurow has pointed out, the system of equity finance and frequent profit reporting leads to an attempt to enhance profits by squeezing wages (Thurow, 1992). This is done:

- by allowing only small increases
- by offsetting them through 'downsizing'
- by moving manufacturing to low-wage countries such as Mexico and Taiwan

By the 1990s in consequence labour contract discussion would centre on benefits, the new battleground, rather than upon wages where gain would be small for the reasons canvassed above. Companies feeling able to be generous would go into the negotiation under the banner of 'no takeaways'; less generous or less well-placed companies would indeed try to chip away at benefits granted in the past, and all this applies especially to medical benefits whose cost continued to spiral. In consequence MHR departments in the 1990s are often significantly involved in attempts to restructure the medical insurance arrangements for their employees, a theme that will be taken up in the following chapter which focuses on the MHR function.

9

Personnel and People

In the present chapter I aim to do two things, connected in a way. First to look at the personnel or MHR function. Second, in the light of the insights offered in previous chapters, and exploiting our European distance from the material, to offer some thoughts on what Europeans going to work for American organisations, in the USA, need to understand, and vice versa. This will not be about do's and don'ts but rather about appreciating the expectations of another culture. But first to personnel.

The personnel function

For anyone seeking to characterise management in another country and to relate management behaviour to the environing society the personnel function is likely to reward close attention. There are several reasons for this.

The most obvious is that the personnel function is a dynamic link between the company and society. It does have an internal operational focus, like the production function or engineering or finance, but that focus is not exclusive. Personnel is concerned with people, their procurement, retention, and also with their training and development. As such it must be concerned with the skills and qualifications that applicants and new entrants possess, and of course with the educational system and its institutions where these have been achieved. But it is broader than this, and personnel managers will also (need to) have a better understanding of the wants, needs and aspirations that people bring to the organisation.

A more focused variation on this theme is to say that the personnel function is often also the company's principal link with the outside world in the sense of the country's national authorities. Personnel tends to be at the receiving end of government initiatives, regulatory controls and new legislation. These considerations are not inconsequential in any country, but as was suggested in the earlier discussion of proactivity as an American virtue they are particularly salient in the USA, where governments believing in the betterment of the human condition seek to advance that end by programmes, initiatives and legislation.

Personnel also tend to develop an internal overview. They hire for finance and for engineering, for the purchasing department and for R & D. Their processing of applicants, employees and even retirees bridges differences in rank and salary level, in departmental and functional allegiance. This does not make managers who work in personnel either omniscient or all wise, but it does give them some claim to generalise about the organisation and its culture.

For these reasons it seems worth having a separate discussion of the personnel function in the USA, and confronting the general question, is this function in America appreciably different from the European equivalent?

Personnel in Europe and America

I would like to suggest that the personnel function is different in the USA, both in a broad and in a diffuse sense, and in some points of detail. The broad difference, in my view, is a higher and more consistent degree of proactivity. And much of the detail difference can be illuminated by responding to the question: what is American personnel proactive about?

Before taking up this question, however, it may be helpful to 'anchor' the dimension of proactivity–reactivity at the negative end. To show that the American proactivity in personnel management alleged here contrasts with something, let us take a European country by way of comparison. On the basis of earlier research I have argued elsewhere that the personnel function in (West) Germany is reactive in a variety of ways (Lawrence, 1982). To take some particular points.

- German personnel managers for the most part neither initiate nor conduct salary negotiations; these take place at a higher level between trade unions and employers' federations; all the company-based personnel managers have to do is implement the results!
- Germany has an elaborate set of labour laws and a system of labour courts; the personnel manager's job is to apply the law.
- While appearance of individual companies in the labour courts is scarcely a daily event, it is a contingency. The German personnel manager will always be asking himself (there are not in my experience many women in this role) how would it look in court?; actions are pre-meditated and at least mentally measured on juridical scales.
- Germany has a co-determination or industrial democracy system dating from the early 1950s; again German personnel managers

need to understand the details of the system, especially regarding the rights and duties of the *Betriebsrat*, or works council.

- A lot of the time and energy of the German personnel manager is taken up with 'servicing' the works council: facilitating its meetings, providing it with information, answering its questions, investigating matters that it has raised.

Is it, indeed, any wonder that the traditional qualification for the German personnel manager has been the Dr Jura, the doctor's degree in Law?

Now the German case probably is at the very reactive end of the continuum, but we would like to argue that America is at the opposite end with other European countries such as Britain in an intermediate position. What then are the Americans proactive about?

Benefits

Certainly, there is a proactive orientation with regard to benefits. The background to this issue is the relatively low level of social welfare benefits provided by the American state in comparison with what is normal in north-west European countries : on the American side of the equation this leaves a lot of slack which traditionally has been taken up by employers. This proactive orientation operates in at least three ways.

First there is corporate initiative in the conceiving of benefits, in devising benefits systems and packages. It is not all straightforward and 'just what you would imagine'; American companies on occasion provide benefits their European counterparts could not readily imagine. Employee assistance programmes, for example, may provide employees and partners with support and/or counselling in such areas as marriage guidance and alcoholism. Companies sometimes have elaborate in-house savings programmes, with tax exemption and an employer contribution, where withdrawals are subject to controls and conditions. Certainly, the golden age of benefits is now past in the USA (as it is in Europe, where it never had the same plenitude and lustre) but in the 1950s and 1960s the quality and extent of such benefits was a competitive weapon for companies in the scramble for manpower during a period of expansion – a slightly more subtle version of being the best payer in the region. Now, as suggested in the previous chapter, it is rather more a question of 'claw-backs' and 'take-aways' but even these offer scope for proactive personnel staff. After all, the aim is to find ways of saving the company money, especially on increasingly expensive medical benefits, but without any unnecessary alienating of the workforce. So one will be looking for alternative insurers/ providers of health care for the workforce, opportunities to get a better deal as a result of concentrating or simplifying the system, or trading off freedom against cost. The import of the latter is that the employees are encouraged to trade off their freedom to use *any* doctor-clinic-hospital-pharmacy, i.e., accept a major principal provider of these services, and in turn do not have the benefits taken away from them or be obliged to pay. Or they retain the original freedom to go anywhere for treatment, but accept 'co-pay', that is, are obliged to make a contribution from their own resources. But notwithstanding the changing times, we should beware of writing off benefits as the bonus of a bygone age. As one of our interviewers put it:

> The question you ask is how can MHR do something for the organis- ation that makes it better. We want a situation where you get a thousand applicants for a job. We want to be the best place to work. If someone like the MHR department is out pushing, it will get done.

Second, quite simply, the administration of the benefits is more important in the USA than in Europe. This again has to be seen against the background of American presupposition. And a cardinal presumption is that workers will not join a trade union if they are treated right – after all, in the American scheme of things there can be no appeal to ideology, class solidarity, or blue-collar traditions. As one of our MHR managers put it in responding to a question about the range of MHR activities:

> We are training managers to be good managers. Union avoidance is achieved by treating people right.

So it matters that the administration of benefits, by personnel, is prompt, efficient and friction free. And it matters more in America than in Europe.

Third there is in the matter of benefits a need for knowledge, for wider knowledge, a need to know what other employers are offering and how their minds are working. To have competitive advantage as an employer in the matter of benefits one needs to be better rather than good: one is measured comparatively rather than absolutely. This particular need for American personnel staff to be widely informed merges into a more general need for information.

What do they think and feel?

It is not really obvious until you have crossed a cultural frontier, but in a country where most places of employment are non-unionised, and where there is no system of industrial democracy, it is much more difficult to get to know about the way employees are thinking and feeling. What is the climate of the workforce, what is morale like, is there 'trouble down at mill' – these are questions that are less easy to answer in America than in many European countries. Of course there is nothing black and white about this. American managers may use their imagination and intuition, 'keep their ears to the ground', talk to employees, 'take soundings', and so on like managers in any country. Yet the fact remains that for the most part they are deprived of *institutional* means of apprehending employee wants and woes. The issue may be underlined by taking Britain as a comparison. In Britain no line manager is ever likely to suffer from ignorance on such matters, if only because shop stewards will line up for the privilege of communicating them.

Again this contrast does impinge on the general matter of proactivity in personnel management in the USA, in the sense that the Americans may well (have to) take steps to probe these entities. Thus, for instance, personnel departments may conduct surveys of employee attitudes, ask about job satisfaction, its converse, and their causes. Or again personnel may institute round table discussions with employees to the same end, but with more interactive and less formal means. This genre of personnel activity in the USA is simple enough, but its existence is not obvious to Europeans.

There is another dimension to this probing and ascertaining activity, and this concerns pay. American companies are more autonomous in the matter of the remuneration they offer. Most of them are not unionised and in any case the preservation of the managerial prerogative is always a priority. So these companies want to take the initiative when it comes to pay, but in the absence, frequently, of representatives of organised labour telling them what workers want, how do they know how much to pay?

The answer again is surveys. Companies need salary data. They need to know what is the industry average, or the locality average, before they can decide how and where to position themselves. Again it is another area of personnel work in the USA that is relatively absent in Europe, where employee representatives and their organisations will take the initiative in matters of salary data, industry and regional variations, pay relativities and remuneration trends.

Union avoidance

Programmes to avoid the workforce becoming trade union members is another form of MHR activity, as indicated in the previous chapter. Most American companies are not unionised. American management is strongly committed to the preservation of the management prerogative, so proaction to exclude trade unions is the natural consequence – and most of the proaction occurs in the MHR area. The measures include:

- a competitive benefits package; or when 'times are hard' at least a package that is not uncompetitive, that compares badly with that offered by other employers
- an efficient administration of benefits; it is important to note that ' Americans expect efficiency, they put their faith in systems and expect them to work; the contrast with the British in this matter is particularly instructive: British people are schooled to expect inefficiency – they get called for jury service when they are in jail, get sent forms they don't need in triplicate, and at the end of the month the janitor gets the CEO's pay slip – fine, everyone enjoys a bit of wry humour
- a remuneration system that is reasonable, competitive, rational and calculable
- to this end, salary surveys or data gathering may be necessary, as suggested earlier
- it is also not uncommon for MHR departments to prepare for employees an itemisation of the benefits they enjoy (to remind them how well off they are) and to drive home the point that union membership could bring nothing extra
- trying to foresee and foretell problems and grievances, and to keep a finger on the pulse of workforce climate, by the means suggested in the previous section
- by training line managers and first line supervisors in union avoidance techniques and grievance handling

Underlying all this, of course, is a purely utilitarian view of unionism – employees will only join unions if they are not treated right, there can be no political or ideological reason.

Not being had
As Geoffrey Gorer pointed out a long time ago (1948) Americans do not like to be had. Gorer rightly draws attention to the paradox that Americans are often conspicuously generous, will give freely on the basis of kindness and decency, but will react more sharply than most people to being had, done, overcharged, cheated and conned.

It is all rather the same with regard to the law and what it enjoins. As we have seen, the American state has rather more confidence than is common in Europe in its ability to shape behaviour through enactment, to achieve betterment through programmes. And again much of the load falls on the MHR function.

A number of examples of this 'being proactive so as not to get caught' have been cited in previous chapters, including:

checking out the position of 'about to be acquired' companies, and any pending lawsuits against them

a concern to (be seen to) implement the Americans with Disabilities Act (1992)

being seen to conform to the equal employment opportunities requirements

likewise, being able to demonstrate an affirmative action plan

MHR departments seem to be particularly sensitive when it comes to equality issues, and on occasion the manifestation of this concern seems extreme to Europeans. In one of the companies visited, for example, employing mostly part skilled white collar personnel, a tour with the MHR-VP included 'the test room'. The skills and/or knowledge bases tested among job applicants in this room were for the most part pretty straightforward things – typing speeds, basic grammar, vocabulary, computer skills and so forth. But the manager concerned was inclined to play down this testing – they did not do it that much, they would not test say all 30 applicants for a secretarial post but just the five who were shortlisted, it was not really central to their selection procedures. When pressed the manager admitted that anyone who fails to get a job they have applied for may turn and accuse the company, perhaps on equal employment opportunity grounds, *and use the test itself as evidence.* That is to say, they will claim that the test is unfair, or that it is culturally biased.

There is probably a wider issue here. Europeans generally perceive American society as being rather more frightening and threatening. After all, by (most) European standards:

- there is more crime
- there is much more violence
- there is less welfare provision by the state
- there is less trade unionism and therefore less traditional protection for ordinary people in the workplace

The counterpoise to all this is American individualism. Individuals have a greater need as well as tendency to be on guard, to look out for themselves, to use in life's struggle any weapons that have been put into their hands, including an appeal to law or the threat of it.

We have selected the personnel function for a closer look for two reasons. It seemed to offer a number of Anglo-American or Euro-American contrasts – attitudes to systems and efficiency, to trade unionism, to litigation, to the provision of benefits, and so on. And at the same time the personnel function seemed to offer further

evidence of American proactivity and that in an area of management work where, as suggested by the German comparison offered
at the beginning, proactivity is by no means guaranteed.

Changing places

This is a 'what it is like' book rather than a 'how to' book, but it
seems a pity to miss the opportunity to offer a few thoughts on what
Europeans going to work in the USA, in American companies, or to
run American subsidiaries of European companies, may find it
helpful to understand, and the reverse of this: Americans going to
work in Europe. This is not exactly a 'need to know' itemisation but
rather some reflections on the differences in management style and
practice and the way these relate to cultural values. These
differences may well impact on the individual.

Going west

The first thing to appreciate is that it will be different. This is not
something that goes without saying. One might well feel that the
canons of professional management together with the dynamics of
business will have such a homogenising effect that while one might
expect to encounter differences in everyday life in America such
differences will be minimal in the office. This is not an unreasonable
viewpoint: business and management are a force for homogeneity,
but not an absolute force, so differences will still be experienced. It
is probably particularly important for British people to take this
expectation of differences on board since the British are often prone
to the idea that common ancestry, the shared language and Atlantic
status, not to mention joint efforts against common foes from Adolf
Hitler to Sadam Hussein, will serve to minimise the difference. They
won't. Indeed precisely because Americans have a strong image of
the British, the latter are likely to have a sense of the difference
projected onto them (whereas Americans will find it easier to
convince themselves that, say, Belgians are 'just like us' really).

Second, many Europeans will feel in the USA that they are
confronted with a more explicit commitment to work in American
companies. There is a lot of coming in early, working late, starting
and ending business journeys at the weekend, coming in at the
weekend, and even special events scheduled at the weekend –
presentations to senior people, task force meetings. American
vacations are also shorter than European ones, and the ensemble of
one-day public holidays is probably less in the USA than it is in
most European countries. Or again, no American will ever go home
for lunch, in the way that say the Swiss and Italians do (apart from

anything else there would not be anyone to go home to). No doubt there is some play-acting here on the part of the Americans, but this will still be a 'presenting reality' for incoming Europeans. Everyone will at least pay lip service to the idea that work-success-achievement comes first.

Third, at an earlier stage I indicated the American predilection for information rather than knowledge. This has two implications for the incoming European. The first is to be cautious about displays of knowledge, of coherent understanding. Such displays may be regarded as somewhere between irrelevant and ostentatious. The second consideration is perhaps more down to earth. This is that where relevant information exists people concerned are expected to have mastered it. Not knowing the facts will carry more 'demerits' in America than in Europe, and there is less tolerance for the European tactic of pretending that mastering the facts is a bit boring and mechanical, and best left to others.

Fourth, American management has a penchant for action. In the situation where it is all so complicated that you cannot possibly tell what is the thing to do, the Europeans may well do nothing for fear of making the situation worse and the Americans will always want to do something. When in his inauguration speech Franklin D. Roosevelt observed that 'the American people want action, and action now' he was expressing a corporate as well as an historical verity. To put it the other way round, Europeans in America may well have to 'lend themselves' to some action, even though the cause and effect relationship has not been established to their satisfaction.

Fifth, American communication is typically an amalgam of explicitness-directness-forceful simplification. As such it is at odds with much European communication: with the painstaking and detailed German exegesis, with Dutch expression of temperate forbearance, with controlled English vagueness, with Italian rotundity. One does not have to converge on the American model (though this will solve a lot of problems) but one must at least be aware of the rules the Americans are playing to. One consequence of this is that European displays of irony, paradox, *double entendre*, wry humour and heavy metaphor are likely to confuse or even dismay an American audience.

Sixth, Europeans will find that systems are more prevalent and evoke more loyalty and esteem. Part of that system penchant is the pervasive desire for quantification. Anything that is quantified seems more real to Americans than anything that is not. Above all, performance should be subject to quantifiable measures in the American scheme of things. The upshot is that Europeans will be confronted by a paradox: American managers are more decisive and exercise less discretion at the same time.

Seventh, when Americans look outside the borders of their country they have a diminished sense of diversity. Other countries seem to them to be either 'just like us' (Canada) or quite indistinguishable from each other (Spain versus Italy, Holland versus Denmark). Europeans need to be prepared for this, and not be disconcerted by it. If you are a Dane there is no reason why you should not feel flattered to hear your capital city Amsterdam praised lavishly. One also needs to be prepared for a bit of benign vagueness about what languages are spoken in these countries.

Eighth, paradoxically, while Americans fail to differentiate outside their borders they do differentiate at home. Their awareness of regional variation within the USA is often strong, and they are offended by foreign presumptions that it is all right to speak about 'you Americans' as though there were no difference between Washington and Jackson, Mississippi. American vagueness about other countries does not prepare the visitor for this sensitivity.

Ninth, there is yet another paradox in American executive behaviour, and this is that American companies will *both* follow the rules more conscientiously and take more risks. To expand this a little, the attachment to systems leads Americans to follow their own procedures to an extent that some Europeans find unimaginative or even slavish. At the same time the attachment to happiness, success and achievement, and the relative freedom from constraint, incline them to bold moves in situations of uncertainty. Europeans tend to get fixated on whichever half of the equation they are exposed to first, and to be bemused by the eventual realisation that both go together.

Tenth, for Americans life is a challenge, to which one responds proactively. Striving is normal, success is something to be openly pursued. There should be some element of risk in all this. You don't bet the farm if all you need to do is bet the pig, but something should be at stake in these strivings. One manifestation of this risk proneness is a disdain for people in jobs from which they cannot get fired. Job security, in the form for instance of the tenured college professor, evokes disdain rather than envy. Or again the maximisation of pleasure is a perfectly legitimate challenge, almost as though you could 'take it with you' (Hemingway's notion of the movable feast). All this play-to-win emphasis is a little disquieting for Europeans, who can readily imagine what it will be like to lose, whereas for Americans, as is emblazoned on a popular T-shirt design:

LOSING IS NOT AN OPTION!

Hallo to all that

For American managers going to work in Europe the issue of cultural migration is compounded by ideological inversion. America, after all, was invented to get away from all that – feudalism, classism, privilege, and ascription. Still, if you have to go, you might as well make them like you!

Diversity really is Europe's most important feature. All the countries are different from each other, as well as from the USA. All those American surveys of international business phenomena that counterpose all aggregated Europe to an integrated Japan and USA are violating reality. The difference between Italy and Norway really is as remarkable as that between France and the USA. What is more, size is not an issue in Europe. Size is not a prerequisite for statehood or national consciousness or cultural identity: Denmark and Switzerland may be smaller than Massachusetts but they are still real, and really different. Neither for the most part are Europeans much impressed by size. Germans are not sobered by the thought that their country might be smaller than Texas (and at the level of material engineering would find much to criticise in Texas). Europeans are more likely to be impressed by the use of space (say the Netherlands), and perhaps by a stature that is disportionate to size – the 'plucky little Belgian' phenomenon of 1914; but size itself is seen as conferring an obligation rather than an advantage.

When Americans see differences between European countries there is a tendency to see these differences in terms of relative closeness to or distance from the American norm, perhaps especially in matters of business and management. This is natural, but wrong. It is not the case that American management represents the one best way, or the only way, notwithstanding the strengths it displays. What Americans will find in Europe is different management styles and practices acted out in different national-institutional contexts, often very different from those of the USA, *but it works for them.* To give a simple if incendiary example, European countries that have a system of industrial democracy are not too dumb to understand the importance of the management prerogative, but having understood it they have still decided to limit it in response to other values.

None of the European countries have the same emphasis on systems-formalisation-SOPs as does the USA. This is not a black and white contrast: countries in Europe have these entities but they lack the centrality and pre-eminence they enjoy in the USA.

In some of these countries, indeed, there are values that run counter to the systems – SOPs emphasis of American management. The Dutch, for example, find too much systems emphasis to be pretentious, claiming too much for the business in hand; the British tend to find it a bit limiting, something for the 'lower downs' while the 'higher ups' will be differentiated by the degree of discretion they enjoy, rather than by their zeal in upholding systems. Or again the Germans will tend to see the systems as no more than an adjunct to the process of design and manufacture, and the French will see some tension between SOPs and cleverness-driven elitism. In short the visiting Americans may find that the respect for systems is tempered by other values.

The commitment of European countries to the notion of leadership is quite variable, but Europe has in common an inclination to view leadership as non-programmable. That is to say, the European understanding of leadership is that it is based on distinctive personal qualities, perhaps including a charismatic element, and that the phenomenon of leadership is difficult both to specify and to inculcate. A practical consequence of this conviction is that there is more variation in Europe, a greater range of type. So there is not an ideal type manager, or business leader, or industrialist in Europe. Again, diversity is the norm.

In Europe, even after the heady managerialist 1980s, business is not the first priority of the nation. Other values compete, and indeed other values intrude on business thinking and strategy. These may variously include national glory, national autarchy, technical virtuosity for its own sake, social responsibility, and cooperation with government. Again at the level of personal deportment there may be other values and models that soften the model of the 'all-American' professional manager – attachment, for instance, to language, to humour, to *culture générale*, to equality norms. These values may be regarded as existential ends rather than as means to ends.

There is in general in Europe more tolerance for idiosyncrasy, eccentricity and individual variance. Or to put it another way there is less focus on 'an approved model'. Goal-related behaviours are similarly less focused. Not all European politicians are glad-handing extroverts and crowd workers, and the expectation that they should be is weaker. Similarly, not all European businesspeople are single-minded and hard driving; not all of them aim to *become* 'a legend in their lifetime', and many may aim to *be* a variety of things.

There is less emphasis in Europe on means to ends. A less instrumental orientation pervades behaviour. Some qualities are esteemed for what they are rather than for what they may lead to, for instance intelligence, education, wit, sophistication, raised consciousness, interiority. The classic American question: 'If you're so smart, why aren't you rich?' is only meaningful to Europeans as an illumination of the American psyche.

There is a paradox in the matter of egalitarianism. The USA is egalitarian by conviction, and the society is marked by an approximate equality of manners – and Europe is thought by Americans to be more elitist-classist-divisive. The Americans are broadly right, but this is not all of the story. The diminished individualism in Europe in the sense of less emphasis on the right to achieve and less lauding of the achievement, implies more respect for others. Or to put it shortly, less emphasis on success means more tolerance for the weak.

To return to the issue of means and ends, there is another difference. Americans incline to the view that the relationship between means and ends, cause and effect, is typically a simple one. Also that it is smart to construe these relationships simply. Indeed part of the attraction of America for Europeans is this American flair for cutting through the anguish and dubiety to a simple dynamic formulation. It is all the other way round for Europeans. They think the world is complex. They have a circumspect view of causality, and do not necessarily see simple means–ends relationships. This circumspection is understandable in societies with a historical legacy of skill, status, culture and suffering.

In the next chapter we will question the legitimacy of this exercise in general characterisation which has been the theme of this book.

10

Audit

Piers Paul Read, the English novelist, explores in one of his books the issue of how institutions are perceived by insiders and outsiders. Regarding Cambridge University he notes that while to outsiders it presents an image of undifferentiated privilege and exclusivity, to insiders it is a finely graded hierarchy. For those on the inside the difference between King's College and, say, Selwyn is greater than that between the universities of Cambridge and Sheffield. Anyone who is writing about management in another country does well to keep such relativities in mind.

In the previous chapters I have sought to offer an overall characterisation of American management, doing this in part with reference to particular qualities – individualism, proactivity, systems and strategy; in the two immediately preceding chapters we have considered primarily a particular phenomenon – employee relations and a specific area of management work, namely personnel – since these seemed to have an indicative quality. But let us return to 'the big picture'.

This overall approach raises a number of questions, one of which has to be: is this kind of treatment justified? It is at this point that Piers Paul Read's two views of Cambridge may be helpful.

Is a general view of American management admissible?

The first problematic one ought to consider here is indeed that posed by Read. If one is American looking around on the inside, one will see primarily difference: the difference between General Motors and the Nashville Wire Company, between a career in sales and work in engineering, between brewing and electronics, between New York City and Holbrook, Arizona, as well as the myriad differences between individual managers as people.

It is part of the career of the teacher of comparative management that one is not without honour, save in one's own country and among one's own people. One can tell one's fellow countrymen about management in France or Germany, Israel or Canada, and they will listen spellbound. But try to offer them a few generalisations about management in Britain and you will be told:

'That's a stereotype.'
'You have oversimplified.'
'It's different in Scotland.'

or better still:

'My boss does not have any of the qualities you have described as typical of this country.'

Fine, but the differentiating insider view does not invalidate the generalising outsider perspective, and the two are reconcilable. More than this, insiders typically have difficulty with 'the big picture', which needs a bit of distance, and a mind ready to receive impressions. On a clear summer's day on the flight from London to Stockholm there is a point at which one can see the whole of Denmark – but you couldn't see the whole of Denmark from the tower of Aarhus Cathedral.

There is another angle, and this is the importance of generalisation as a framework for understanding. Generalisation is the means by which we advance. The generalisation can be qualified, but not substituted. The big picture precedes the small picture, the telescope comes before the microscope. This formulation is well recognised within a community, whether national or scientific, where 'work that breaks new ground' is always welcomed, whatever revision may be seen as desirable subsequently. This conviction is not jeopardised when international boundaries are crossed. Only generalisation can bridge the gap between our experience of the world and our understanding of it.

But in the case of American management a certain paradox intrudes: the paradox of individualism. How, that is, can one characterise American management in general terms while at the same time asserting, as I have done, that individualism is a key feature? Would not that same individualism be a force for divergence and difference, a force for a heterogeneity beyond generalisation? This is a fair question, and it does raise the issue of individualism in relation to nationality.

The conventional approach here is to treat individualism as a dependent variable, as in propositions of the kind: the French are more inclined to be individualistic than the Swedes. Propositions of this kind are perfectly meaningful, they may well be true, and one can envisage some kinds of evidence. At the same time, I would like to argue something a little different.

If we take Hofstede's famous study (Hofstede, 1991) and consult its individualism table it emerges that the countries with the highest scores for individualism are the Anglo-Saxon countries, led by the

USA! Fine, it is nice to have some friendly support for the case argued in this book. But does the Hofstede table tell us anything else? Well, it certainly suggests that whatever measures or indicators were used they were favourable to the Anglo-Saxon countries. And since there is no suggestion that Hofstede tried to stack the cards, it may be that there is a certain kind of individualism that is manifest to a greater or lesser degree in all the Anglo-Saxon countries, with America in the lead. But are there other versions of individuality, versions not degrees, rooted in different national cultures?

Again the Hofstede table is instructive here. In tenth place is France. Now not only might some people, including 50 million Frenchmen, quibble at France ranking *after* the Anglo-Saxon countries, but worse is yet to come. France is not just in tenth place, but in *joint* tenth place. And the country with which it jointly shares the honour is – Sweden!

Now it need hardly be said that this finding runs counter to popular opinion. The commonly held view, that is, is that Sweden is restrained and conformist, but that France is irrepressible and individualist. So there must be different versions of individuality and the French version is clearly not being 'captured' by whatever means Hofstede used, such that France comes behind England in the individualism stakes, and merely 'breaks even' with Sweden.

So what, then, might be the difference between French and American individualism, given that both countries are popularly credited with strong individualism? Certainly when the question is posed in this way one can see behavioural differences between the two peoples, and the next question is about how one might generalise these differences.

One possibility is to distinguish between being and becoming. American individualism is about becoming – the best or the biggest, the first or the fastest, the richest or most renowned. Whereas French individualism is expressive, and what it expresses is a differentiated state of being – via taste, choice, style, wit, and on occasions in behaviour that is not constrained. No American is ever going to put a lead on his pet lobster and take it for a walk, not even in Greenwich Village – but it has been done in Paris.

In other words American individualism has a striving, achieving quality, rather than an expressive and differentiating quality. So Americans may be strongly individualist and mildly conformist at the same time. That is to say, the desire to achieve, to succeed, co-exists with a fairly limited range of objectives. So individualism is not in the American case a force for heterogeneity, as it is in France, and this individualism may indeed form part of a *general* characterisation.

Regionalism

The previous section argued that there is no serious tension between American individualism and an outsider attempt to generalise about American management. But what about regional differences? Americans themselves are very much aware of these differences, and tend, understandably, to resent outsider formulations that seem to view America as a seamless garment. But are these putative regional differences of an economic nature, or are they at least differences likely to impact on the occupational structure?

The answer to this question has to be yes. First and most simply there are substantial differences in income from state to state. The *Statistical Abstract of the United States* for 1994 gives the average per capita income for 1993 in current dollars as $20,817 (US average). But the differences between the states are marked:

Connecticut	$28,110
New Jersey	$26,967
New York	$24,623

At the other end of the scale we have:

Arkansas ⎱	
Louisiana ⎰	$16,143
Mississippi	$14,894

And it is easy to track differences of this magnitude, going back over a quarter of a century.

Of course, there are significant regional differences in the location of industry, type of industry, and ratios of industrial sector versus agricultural and service sector employment. So both the structure and the content of blue collar and white collar workforces vary on a regional basis.

The differences in levels of educational attainment also turn out to vary considerably on a regional basis. Taking again the *Statistical Abstract of the United States* for 1994, as of 1990 the proportion of the whole population with a bachelor's degree is 13.1 per cent. But as with income there are significant differences between states:

Bachelors degree, 1990	(%)
Colorado	18.0
Connecticut	16.2
District of Columbia	16.1
Massachusetts	16.6
Minnesota	15.6

but at the other end of the scale:

Arkansas	8.9
West Virginia	7.5

A similar pattern is observable for higher degrees, with big differences between states, even though some of the players have changed. The 1990 USA average is 7.2 per cent. At the top are:

District of Columbia	17.2
Connecticut	11.0
Maryland	10.9
Massachusetts	10.6

And at the other end of the scale are:

Alabama	5.5
Idaho	5.3
Mississippi	5.1
South Dakota	4.9
West Virginia	4.8
North Dakota	4.5
Arkansas	4.5

As shown in the introductory chapter, there are substantial lifestyle and consumer pattern differences on an area basis, though for these purposes the state is far too large an entity, and it has been argued that the zip code is a more appropriate unit for this lifestyle analysis.

In short, regional difference is not merely some folksy or residual phenomenon in the USA. It is a concept that appears to be meaningful in terms of income and occupational and educational structure, as well as with regard to lifestyle. But even so, the question remains: does regional difference impact on management practice and values, the subject of this book?

I would like to argue that although the concept of region has demonstrable substance it has little or no impact on management itself, even if the kind of entity that is managed varies regionally.

One reason for this judgement is my own study. While some universal sources were used, the study depended heavily on field-work in the form of company visits and manager interviews, and this was done in several widely different parts of the USA. I could see no difference in management in these various parts of the USA, however much the regions may have differed in economic structure and in other ways.

There is really only one qualification to be made. One of the areas of the study was Texas. In this case it could fairly be said that the rhetoric was more gung-ho, the style more swashbuckling, occasionally bordering on the lawless. On one occasion I was shown round a plant in Texas by the owner-manager, who evinced a certain pride in the life-threatening features of his workplace. His wry comment was:

'If this had been California the EPA [Environmental Protection Agency] would have closed us down three times over'

Colourful though some of this Texan rhetoric was it probably stops short of being a meaningful departure from the American management norm.

A second reason for doubting the impact of regional difference upon management is that there are a number of identifiable forces that are likely to neutralise any regional influence in this sphere. These would include:

- the high presumptive rate of social mobility
- high geographic mobility
- strong and explicit norms of management professionalism
- strong national-value commitment to efficiency
- widespread individual commitment to success and achievement
- high inter-company mobility

The operation of a lot of these forces was illustrated in the manager biographies cited in Chapter 3. It was also argued in the previous section that American individualism tends to reinforce rather than undermine (a trans-regional) homogeneity.

Another reason for concluding that regional difference has little impact upon management practice is that this is what Americans themselves say when asked to confront the issue. I have put the question to a number of managers and management academics in the USA, and the consensus seems to be that management practice and values are trans-regional. The only counter-argument this questioning has thrown up is the line that region/community may affect company success/adaptability. The argument is usually construed negatively and goes like this.

A company already established in region A moves to region B or sets up a works or subsidiary there. This will typically be to get away from rust-belt labour unionism, to benefit from regionally lower wage rates, or to enjoy the benefits of a greenfield site. But then things go wrong – human or social things. The labour force turn out to be less amenable than had been hoped, or particular skills are not locally available. Or the executives find the new location not to their (or their families') liking – lacking in recreational infrastructure or too unsophisticated. And while the testimonies I have been given have for the most part been negative, this phenomenon must have worked positively as well, classically with Silicon Valley, and also with some of the 1990s growth cities in the south-west – Phoenix, Albuquerque and Houston.

A homogeneous style?

In the previous chapters I have constructed a picture of American management in terms of its individualism and professionalism, its penchant for systems and strategy, and its communication style. But am I entitled to treat this style as homogeneous on a person-to-person basis?

I would like to suggest that such a presumption of homogeneity is more legitimate in the American case than it would be for most other countries. The same factors that I suggested earlier transcend regional differences, particularly social and geographic mobility and strong achievement norms, also tend to homogenise society at large.

At the same time in the interviews and discussions with American managers there was some evidence of what one might call a minority strand, a brand of management that was more down to earth, more cynical-critical, more inclined to reflect the popular view of good and bad and less inclined to embrace management rhetoric.

The homespun manager

Part of the homespun style is a dispensing with conceptual complexities; as one interviewed CEO volunteered:

> When I give seminars at university, they ask: Do you have a five year plan? Yes, I reply, in five years' time I want to be in business

Or again:

> Here big corporate names have gotten into trouble because they have not minded the store. We have a bright future so long as we mind the store.

This assertion of simplicity easily shades into criticism of 'the professional manager ethos'. Here, for example, is another executive responding to a question as to whether American management has any obvious shortcomings:

> Sure, CEOs who are too much on the make – stock option plans and all that. Where their philosophy is I, me and myself.

Or again:

> These companies that take benefits away; they should not have given them in the first place. [That is, the honest man will be guided by consistency rather than expediency.]

Or again:

> It is too short-sighted; there is too much of how much we can make in the short term – the Japanese are not like this. We need to win the war as well as the battle.

This last criticism, of short-termism, was in fact quite widespread; probably the majority of the managers I interviewed would articulate some version of this view – with a little prompting. But 'homespun manager' likes to make it a simple axiom.

Another dimension is an inclination to straightforward, decent dealings with others, the 'golden rule' being preferred to professional formulations:

> Leadership works best if managers set a good example.

Or:

> I come in early and stay reasonably late. Employees get a sense of comfort if they see the boss's car there when they get to work and it is still there when they leave. If I leave at noon on Friday they know I am only playing golf, and they are still working.

Or: 'You gotta walk the walk, as well as talk the talk.'

Another executive asked about his report-to's (immediate subordinates) listed them, but then thought it important to add: 'But the door stays open all the time. And I believe in MBWA.' And attention to detail is important, especially 'good-example setting' detail:

> This is a food factory. You have to keep it clean. When I walk around I pick up rubbish and put it in the can. Now everyone does it.

In short, side by side with the dominant professionalised style depicted in earlier chapters, a 'minority strand' exists, emphasising old-fashioned honesty, simplicity, and the power of example. It eschews (the excesses of) professional managerialism, and relishes a bit of condemnation of the guilty – especially those who fail to 'walk the walk'.

An interesting speculation is where this 'minority strand' comes from, and it seems to have no obvious correlates. If one can imagine this scenario transferred to Britain it would be straightforward, a case of 'grafters' versus 'college boys'. But in the USA one has to work pretty hard to find a manager who is not a college boy. Certainly the homespun managers tend to be older rather than younger, and certainly not 'fresh out of college'. But by no means all of the older managers are of the homespun persuasion. Perhaps it is best understood as a perpetuation, on however narrow a front, of

America's much mythologised wholesome past. A management equivalent of the 'straight shooter' in politics.

How professional?

Next I would like to raise the question, is American management professional? It should be said straight away that this is not the same as asking if American management is *a* profession. The professions are usually defined in terms of:

> long and arduous training
> a body of knowledge to be mastered and applied
> loyalty to professional norms, and perhaps obedience to some external regulatory body

Now while one can make some kind of a case in these terms in favour of management being a profession, there are substantial qualifications:

- the nature and duration of training is variable
- the body of knowledge is highly variable in terms of the industry, and of the function (type of management work)
- the knowledge is only part of it, and more important are various human qualities such as leadership, social and political skills, the ability to communicate and motivate, and so on
- the primary loyalty is to the employing organisation

Moreover, these qualifications apply rather more strongly to management in the USA than they would in Europe. American management tends to be generalist rather than specialist in its orientation. It puts its faith in the operation of systems rather than in the specialist knowledge that might have originated them. And the generalism is to no small degree fuelled by the human qualities – drive and organisational skills – rather than by the possession of transferable knowledge. American companies are also likely to be more demanding of their management employees than are European ones.

In short it is always rather questionable as to whether or not management is best described as a profession, and that formulation is particularly difficult to sustain in the case of American management. But is it professional?

Professional in what sense? In the sense of being the opposite to amateur. In the sense of taking the activity set and its objectives seriously, in the sense of playing to win. Clearly in this sense American management is very professional. But is there more to the argument?

Certainly there are a number of strands to it. First there is a seriousness of purpose; it is embedded in the individualism explored in Chapter 3 and in the general emphasis in American culture on success and personal achievement. This seriousness of purpose impacts strongly on American management, which is invariably powerful and focused – not playful, not negligent, and not amateur.

Most importantly, the systems and standard operating procedures are the apparatus of professionalism. They represent the American attempt to streamline, standardise, capture, control and to maximise efficiencies. Much of what American managers, indeed American companies, achieve is achieved by means of their systems (rather than through acts of individual creativity or performance). When people from other countries speak of American companies as being well run, of Americans as being organised and efficient, the implicit reference is to the efficiency of their systems. A 'typical well-run American company' is well run because these systems are in place, and respected.

The American concern with strategy puts this professionalism on a higher plane. This is not simply an operational professionalism, but a professionalism that goes beyond time present, and is concerned with perpetuation and continuity, with a middle-term attempt to configure the activities of the company and to manipulate the relationship between the company and its environment to facilitate the future achievement of profitability.

Finally the strain towards proactivity – the opposite of *laissez-faire*, of wait and see, of simply 'mind the store' and hope for the best – suffuses American managerial behaviour, giving it a tone of self-conscious striving. This puts American management at one end of a scale: fatalism is at the other end. We are not concerned here with the will of Allah, but with the resolve of corporate vice-presidents!

Judge and jury?

There is a qualification to the judgement I have made in the previous section. This is that I have judged American management by standards it has itself originated rather than by some objective standards that exist independently. To 'space out' this argument a little one would have to say that it is American practice and the American management literature that have given us a concept of professional management in the first place, and so in no small degree we are making inferences from a classic American formulation of what is right for managers and companies, and then measuring what we have seen in American companies in the 1990s against these standards. In short, the exercise is a little circular. Does this matter? Probably not. It is not a reason to 'take marks off'. It would make at least as good sense to credit America both for formulating the standards and for living up to them. If there is a danger this concerns rather the attempt to judge *other* countries by these American standards, an enterprise that tends to deny the inevitable connection in any society between management behaviour and macro socio-cultural values. So that in its crude form a certain 'managerial imperialism' may emanate from the USA whereby Americans apply their model to other societies, and they find them wanting to the extent that they do not conform to this model. To give a firm example (or two), management in both France and Germany is very different from management in the USA. But the styles, presumptions, behaviours of French and German managers reflect different socio-cultural values, relate to different national institutions, are shaped by different histories. And 'it works for them'.

11

An American Paradox

In the Kimbell Art Museum in Fort Worth, Texas there is a picture by James Ensor, an avant-garde Belgian painter of the late nineteenth century, that depicts some skeletons. All of them are dressed and one is even wearing a top hat. They are grouped colourfully and with compositional balance around a brazier. The picture is entitled *Skeletons Warming Themselves*.

What does this have to do with an evaluation of American management? Well, a dominant theme in the last quarter of the twentieth century has been the economic decline of the USA. While the USA is among the very richest countries of the world, and is certainly the world's mightiest economy, it has experienced and been very conscious of undergoing a *relative* economic decline.

This is a relative decline in two senses. First it is a decline relative to America's own past. It no longer has the effortless economic superiority it enjoyed for a quarter of a century or so after the Second World War. Incremental rises of GNP per capita have continued but since the post-war golden age the USA has also experienced:

- a loss of international markets
- a loss of leadership in certain industries
- massive de-industrialisation, in part springing from lack of competitiveness; a quarter of a million jobs in manufacturing are being lost each year in the 1990s according to one writer (Henwood, 1994)
- some loss of domestic markets
- change from being an investor nation to being an investee – a country in which others invest

Second, and overlapping with the diachronic decline, is a decline relative to other countries and regions, especially Western Europe and Japan. The USA may still be richer than these areas, but it is no longer *massively* richer, as it once was. The difference between say Belgium and the USA is not significant: it will not shape a European world view (or cause massive emigration to the USA). In the 1950s and 1960s Europe saw millions of American tourists, while only rich Europeans or senior executives ever visited the USA. But now

Europeans routinely visit the USA – for north-west Europe the USA as a holiday destination is simply an alternative to the Mediterranean.

Furthermore, European companies now buy American companies (something that would have been unthinkable in the 1950s). British banks buy mini-chains in the USA. European airlines look for 'second tier' American ones they can buy into, aiming at code-sharing deals and plugging into American hubs. Japan has become the American government's creditor; Germany exports more than the USA. Lots of countries, not just Germany and Japan, have a favourable trade balance with America. Economically speaking America used to be a country that 'did it' to others; now it is a country that has it 'done to them'. Or as Robert Waterman of *In Search of Excellence* fame put it in a mid-1990s book (Waterman, 1994): 'If we are doing so well, why does it feel so bad?' $\quad$ 658. 00973

Back at this point to James Ensor's skeletons 'warming them-selves': in the light of this relative but emotionally poignant decline, does it make sense to praise American management for its professionalism, or are its practitioners forlornly ensconsed before the fire, as in Ensor's picture?

It is the purpose of this book to offer a portrait of American management, not to analyse the causes of relative economic decline. But even so, it is fair to ask if this decline is occurring because of American management, or in spite of it.

American management and economic decline

Has American management caused this decline? The answer has to be no. The American management establishment has provided the world with standards of efficiency and effectiveness – and for the most part lived up to them itself. Has American management then in any way contributed to this decline?

To this narrower question one has to return a qualified yes. In the matter of short-termism American management is passively culpable: at the end of the day 'they bought it'.

By short-termism is meant the American concern (obsession) with profits in the short run, monitored at short-term intervals, namely quarterly. When these short-term profits are not forthcoming, when there is something like 'two bad quarters', then the tendency is to take decisive (and negative) action: downsize, cut training, cut benefits, withdraw from unprofitable product-markets, cut the R & D spend, and let 'heads roll'. In short to do a number of things that make it pretty unlikely that the company concerned will ever win again.

These short-term strategy moves have been particularly damaging in the USA's industrial sector by sector battles with Japan. The scenario goes like this. Japan invades an American market with a product that is probably a bit better and certainly a bit cheaper. It makes headway, quite quickly. American manufacturers lose market share – and profit. They withdraw, in theory to concentrate on more profitable areas; then the Japanese clean up!

Played according to these rules it is bound to be an uneven contest. It is like a game of chess where the American contestant is mandated to win in 15 minutes or else be designated the loser, but where the Japanese contestant is simply told to win eventually, no matter how long it takes.

American management must have some responsibility for this organised competitive disadvantage. While it is true that the impulse may come from shareholders and their presumptive demands, there is a senior executive level where management, financers and share-holders overlap and intermingle, where senior executives do not seem to have 'fought their corner' for sensible and middle-term strategies of defence.

This critical point can be reformulated in a more general way, albeit one in which American management is passively rather than actively responsible. There is a certain parallel between the man-agerial individualism portrayed in this book, and economic doctrines favouring free enterprise, the maximising of competition, the separation of government and industry, and of companies and banks. Yet it has been argued by for instance Lester Thurow (1992) that at least two of America's rivals – Japan and Germany – are operating a system of 'commutarian capitalism' rather than of classic American capitalism. That is to say, both these countries have benefited from a modification of free enterprise purity, have allowed their companies a degree of security as a result of cross-shareholding, have encouraged debt finance (long-term funding by banks), rather than equity finance (funding by shareholders), and have functional educational systems and especially vocational education that has really served industry.

Our competing, achieving, individualising American manager is unlikely to lobby for such developments as these.

Education and decline

Again, it might fairly be asked if our study of American manage-ment has thrown any light on the causes of decline, even if this were not the object of the research. Certainly it has illuminated one cause, that of the consequences of educational failure.

Educational weakness is one dimension in the explanation of American decline. At the same time it is important to recognise fairly American educational achievements. The USA produces more graduate engineers and scientists than any other country, more people who have studied business administration at college, more MBAs, and more PhDs. Further, a larger proportion of the age group enjoys a college education, even if standards are not uniform, than in any other country in the world. These are redoubtable achievements. So what does America do wrong?

The general charge is weaknesses in primary and secondary education, where standards do not match those of other advanced countries. Both American educational soul-searching and internationally comparative studies suggest in particular:

- high rates of illiteracy, and this among native English-speaking Americans
- poor attainment in maths and science
- poor general knowledge
- little aptitude for foreign languages
- weaknesses in historical and geographical knowledge

One should add to this the virtual absence of vocational education – apprenticeship, training in craft skills relevant to manufacture, job-related training for foremen and technicians, and so on – in the European tradition.

All this has been said before. What emerged in this study was a myriad of confirmations and illustrations of the impact of these deficiencies in American companies. I was told, for instance, that blue collar workers and their supervisors could not do simple maths, could not work out percentages, did not understand the difference between the mean and the average, could not 'keep the score' on scrap rates, did not have the educational resources to implement quality improvement programmes, and were sometimes handicapped by simple illiteracy.

This lower-level educational problem can be put into a wider context. One of the themes of this book has been the American penchant for systems. This origination and administration of systems is a strength, and a nationally distinctive one. It undoubtedly facilitates economies of effort and efficiencies in resource utilisation. Yet it might be argued that at least at some levels these systems are a necessary correction to educational weakness.

The game seems to have changed. In the golden age of American manufacturing, supremacy was taken for granted, markets were vast, volumes more substantial, and exploiting economies of scale was a significant competitive advantage. The well qualified graduates of the

higher education system powered R & D and new product development. An army of industrial engineers fashioned efficient systems
(that 'any idiot' could operate).

But now it has changed. We have market segmentation and
customisation. Shorter product runs, an emphasis on differentiation,
on model change, on shortening the lag between design and
production, on time-based competition. Authority is being pushed
downwards, initiative and adaptability demanded of the workforce;
multi-skills not systems familiarity is the order of the day. Quality
has become the competitive weapon, and the battle for quality has
to be won on the shop floor rather than in the design office.

None of this plays to American strengths.

Diversity

A European viewpoint would suggest that the management of
diversity is becoming increasingly important. And central to this is
the challenge of managing cultural diversity, in the sense of
managing cross-border operations and simultaneously serving
product markets in many countries.

American management has not been seriously challenged in this
respect in the past. The domestic market is so huge that the
internationalising imperative is weaker. The USA is at the opposite
end of the spectrum from European countries such as Sweden,
Switzerland or the Netherlands in this matter. On an earlier
assignment in Sweden I was told repeatedly by senior executives:

> We think of our home markets as being Scandinavia/Western Europe/
> Europe!

There is no American equivalent to this.

On the other hand American companies did internationalise early,
many US companies becoming household names in Britain, for
instance, in the inter-war period. But this internationalisation has
not typically been accompanied by cultural or managerial adaptation to other countries. Rather these companies, as was suggested
in the first chapter, went forth as 'full blooded' American corporations, exported their style, systems and assumptions. And again for
the most part these have been accepted in other countries, and
indeed have earned respect and engendered loyalty among non-
American employees.

In these operations American companies have in the past been
playing a winning hand, doing things on a big scale and doing them
well.

All this has changed. There are more non-American competitors at country level and at corporate level. In many branches of industry there are challenges: Mars is challenged by Nestlé, Anheuser Busch (Budweiser) is challenged by Heineken, General Motors by Toyota, McDonnel Douglas by Airbus, and at a different level NAFTA is challenged by the EU – the latest designation for the ever expanding European common market.

So like it or not, American companies are going to be confronted with more non-American companies. They face stronger inter-nationalising imperatives, they will increasingly have to operate in other countries in an adaptive rather than dominant mode, they will be party to more cross-border mergers and to more cross-border strategic alliances, where they will have to adapt, compromise and negotiate, not simply export the American way – however successful this was in the post-war era.

Running through all this is the theme of cultural relativity and the challenge of managing diversity. These play to American blind spots rather than to American strengths. But this challenge has to be met for America to advance in the wider world.

Bibliography

Barsoux, Jean-Louis (1993) *Funny Business*, Cassell, London.

Barzini, Luigi (1977) *O America: When You and I Were Young*, Harper & Row, New York.

Baudrillard, Jean (1988) *America*, Verso, London.

Berton, Pierre (1986) *Why We Act Like Canadians*, McClelland & Stewart, Toronto

Blackburn, Joseph D. (1991) *Time Based Competition*, Richard Irvin, Homewood, Illinois.

Bloom, Helen *et al.* (1994) *Euromanagement,* Kogan Page, London.

Bluestone, Barry and Harrison, Bennett (1982) *The Deindustrialisation of America* Basic Books, New York.

Bryson, Bill (1989) *The Lost Continent*, Secker & Warburg, London.

Bryson, Bill (1994) *Made in America*, Secker & Warburg, London.

Bull, Andy (1993) *Coast to Coast: A Rock Fan's Tour*, Black Swan (Transworld Publishers), London.

Calori, Roland and De Woot, Phillipe (eds) (1994) *A European Management Model* Prentice Hall, Hemel Hempstead.

Capoe, Joe (1990) *Futurescope*, Longman Financial Services, New York.

Cochran, Thomas C. and Miller, William (1942) *The Age of Enterprise*, Macmillan London and New York.

Collins, James and Porras, Jerry (1994) *Built to Last: Successful Habits of Visionary Companies*, Harper Collins, New York.

Coltrane, Robbie (1993) *Coltrane in a Cadillac*, Fourth Estate, London.

Davies, Pete (1992) *Storm Country*, William Heinemann, London.

Dertouzos, Michael L. *et al.* (1989) *Made in America*, MIT Press, Cambridge Massachusetts.

Drucker, Peter F. (1966) *The Effective Executive*, Harper & Row, New York.

Flood, John (1985) *The Legal Profession in the United States*, American Bar Foundation, Chicago.

Fussell, Paul (1989) *Wartime: Understanding and Behaviour in the Second World War* Oxford University Press, New York.

Fussell, Paul (1991) *Bad or the Dumbing of America*, Simon & Schuster, New York

Garreau, Joel (1981) *The Nine Nations of North America*, Avon Books, New York.

Goldsmith, Olivia (1992) *The First Wives Club*, William Heinemann, London.

Gorer, Geoffrey (1948) *The Americans*, Cresset Press, London.

Hayes, Robert H. and Abernathy, William (1980) 'Managing our Way to Economic Decline', *Harvard Business Review*, July–August, pp. 67–77.

Henwood, Doug (1994) *The State of the USA Atlas*, Penguin Books, Harmondsworth

Hofstede, Geert (1991) *Cultures and Organisations*, McGraw Hill UK, London.

Hoggart, Simon (1990) *America: A User's Guide*, Collins, London.

Hughes, Robert (1993) *Culture of Complaint*, Oxford University Press, London.

Jamieson, Ian (1980) *Capitalism and Culture*, Gower Press, Aldershot.

Jamieson, Ian (1985) 'The American Company in Britain', in P.A. Lawrence and K.E. Elliott (eds), *Introducing Management*, Penguin, Harmondsworth.

Kanter, Rosabeth Moss (1977) *Men and Women of the Corporation*, Basic Books, New York.

Kanter, Rosabeth Moss (1984) *The Change Masters*, Allen & Unwin, London.

Keneally, Thomas (1992) *The Place Where Souls are Born: A Journey into the American South West*, Hodder & Stoughton, London.

Kennedy, Gavin (1987) *Negotiate Anywhere*, Arrow Books, London.

Kiam, Victor (1986) *Going For It*, Collins, London.

Kidder, Tracy (1981) *The Soul of a Machine*, Avon Books, New York.

Kronzucker, Dieter (1989) *Das amerikanische Jahrhundert*, Wilhelm Heyne Verlag, Munich.

Lawrence, Peter (1980) *Managers and Management in West Germany*, Croom Helm, London.

Lawrence, Peter (1982) *Personnel Management in West Germany: Portrait of a Function*, report to the International Institute of Management, West Berlin.

Lawrence, Peter (1984) *Management in Action*, Routledge & Kegan Paul, London.

Lawrence, Peter (1986) *Invitation to Management*, Basil Blackwell, Oxford.

Lawrence, Peter (1991) *Management in the Netherlands*, Oxford University Press, Oxford.

Lawrence, Peter and Spybey, Tony (1986) *Management and Society in Sweden*, Routledge & Kegan Paul, London.

Levering, Robert and Moskowitz, Milton (1993) *The Hundred Best Companies to Work for in America*, Doubleday, New York.

Lewis, Michael (1989) *Liar's Poker*, Hodder & Stoughton, London.

Locke, Robert (1993) 'The Limits of America's Pax Oeconomica: Germany and Japan after World War II', in conference proceedings *Management and the Professions*, University of Stirling, Scotland.

Moore, J.L. (1992) *Writers on Strategy and Strategic Management*, Penguin, Harmondsworth.

Newman, Katherine S. (1988) *Falling from Grace*, Random House, New York.

Oakley, Giles (1976) *The Devil's Music: A History of the Blues*, BBC Books, London.

O'Rourke, P.J. (1988) *Holidays in Hell*, Pan Books/Picador, London.

Patterson, James and Kim, Peter (1992) *The Day America Told the Truth*, Plume (The Penguin Company).

Porter, Michael (1990a) 'The Competitive Advantage of Nations', *Harvard Business Review*, March–April, pp. 73–93.

Porter, Michael (1990b) *The Competitive Advantage of Nations*, The Free Press, New York.

Potter, David, M. (1954) *People of Plenty*, University of Chicago Press, Chicago.

Raban, Jonathan (1981) *Old Glory*, Collins, London.

Raban, Jonathan (1991) *Hunting Mr Heartbreak*, Pan Books, London.

Ramsey, Douglas K. (1987) *The Corporate Warriors*, Grafton Books, New York.

Reich, Robert B. (1990) 'Who is US?', *Harvard Business Review,* January–February, pp. 53–64.

Reid, Peter C. (1990) *Well Made in America*, McGraw Hill, New York.

Servan-Schreiber, J.J. (1967) *Le Défi Américain*, Denvel, Paris.

Soutty, Andy (1993) *The Drive-Thru Museum*, Impact Books, London.

Tanner, Dwight (1994) 'Management in Canada: a Characterisation', PhD thesis, University of Loughborough, Loughborough.

Thurow, Lester (1992) *Head to Head*, William Morrow, New York.

Vernon, Raymond (1980) 'Gone are the Cash Cows of Yesteryear', *Harvard Business Review*, November–December, pp. 150–155.

Waller, Robert James (1993) *The Bridges of Madison County*, Mandarin Paperbacks, London.

Waller, Robert James (1994) *Slow Waltz in Cedar Bend*, Heinemann, London.

Waterman, Robert H. (1994) *The Frontiers of Excellence*, Nicholas Brealey Publishing, London.

Weiss, Michael J. (1988) *The Clustering of America*, Harper & Row, New York.

Whittington, Richard (1993) *What is Strategy – and Does it Matter?*, Routledge, London.

Wriston, Walter B (1990) 'The State of American Management', *Harvard Business Review*, January–February, pp. 78–83.

Index

Abernathy, William 31–2
achievement 7, 111, 120
    and ascription 82
    in Europe 114
    and individuality 117
    and information 11
acquisitions 31
    and drug screening 66
    and lawsuits 67, 91–2, 108
    and self-interest 90–1
action, demand for 110
advantage, competitive
    employee 46, 100
    national 20–2, 30, 33
    and proactivity 65–70, 105
advertising, targeted 15
Affirmative Action Programme 69,
    108
agriculture, and business 22
air transport 30
Algasco 18
Americans, working in Europe
    112–14
Americans with Disabilities Act (1992)
    68, 108

banks
    US/British 76–8
    US/Canadian 7
Barclays Bank Country Report 28, 29
being, and becoming 82, 117
benefits
    and contract negotiation 83, 94, 97,
        99–101
    and proactivity 104–5, 107
Berton, Pierre 6
Boston Consulting Group 54
Britain
    banking 76–7
    industrial relations 9, 99–100, 106,
        107

management 2, 113
manufacturing 34
    and US subsidiaries 72–3
Britons, working in USA 109–11
business, and freedom 7–10

Canada, compared with USA 1–2, 5–7,
    111
capitalism, communitarian 34, 128
car rental 30, 43
career
    and individualism 40–3, 46–7
    and mobility 43–6
change, organisational 74
character, American 1
checking, and communication 84–5
class
    absence of barriers 4, 41, 81–2
    and unionism 93, 94
closure, explicit 65, 84
Collins, James 62
communication 81–90, 110
    and checking 84–5
    and clarity 82–4
    and euphemisms 88–90
    and European comparisons 110
    and hierarchy 85–8
    and zappy speech 90–2
constraint, freedom from 8, 111
contracts, labour 45–6, 83, 95, 96,
    99–102
control systems, and information
    15–16
corporations, size 49
costing, systems 77
craft ideal, and systems 79
credit cards 30
culture, and diversity 130
customers, targeting 15, 63

de-industrialisation 126

de-layering 63, 99
decision-making
   and information 15–16
   and proactivity 64
   shared 9
   strategies 58–60
   and systems 73
decisiveness 7, 10, 71, 79–80, 111
Declaration of Independence 7
deference, and hierarchy 64, 85–8
Dekker, Wisse 22, 28
democracy, industrial 8–10, 97–8,
      103–4, 112
Dertouzos, Michael L. *et al.* 33–4
detail, attention to 57, 122
development, industrial, and strategy
      55–6
difference
   in business cultures 109–14, 115–17
   regional 118–21
differentiation, product 51, 130
directness
   American 81–2, 110
   and euphemism 88–90
   and France 3
diversity
   European 30, 111, 112, 113
   management of 130–1
Drucker, Peter 61
drugs, screening for 66
dynamism
   and strategy 53
   and systems 78–9

economies of scale 49, 53
economy
   and decline xii, 31–2, 33–6, 126–30
   history 20–2
   substance 22–3, 34
   see also manufacturing; resources;
         service sector; trade
education
   and economic decline 128–30
   management 3, 128
   regional differences 118–19
   vocational 129
efficiency 85, 107–8, 128
   and systems 4, 34, 78–9, 80, 124
egalitarianism
   and Europe 114

   and information 11
   and systems 79
employment
   and equality of opportunity 67, 108
   in manufacturing 29
   security 111
   in service sector 29
Ensor, James 126, 127
environmentalism, commitment to 69
equality
   gender 68–9
   of opportunity 67, 82, 108
euphemisms 64, 88–90
Europe
   Americans working in 112–14
   investment in USA 127
   US attitudes towards 111, 112
   and US management systems 4
Europeans, working in USA x, 109–11
exports
   Canadian 5
   diversity 23
   European 127
   and natural resources 35
   and service sector 29–30
   substance 23–8

familiarity, and perceptions of USA x–xi
fast food chains 30
finance
   equity/debt 100, 128
   joint stock 20–1
France
   and individualism 3, 116, 117
   management 203
   and USA 4–5, 34, 113, 125
Franklin, Benjamin 61
freedom
   and business 7–10
   as US value 1, 6–7

generalisation, and differentiation
      115–17
Germany
   economy 34, 35
   and industrial democracy 9, 97–8,
         103–4
   management 2, 113, 125
   and personnel management 103–4
   trade unionism 93, 103

Gimbel, John 37
Gorer, Geoffrey 107
government
    and human resource management 102
    and proactivity 68–70

happiness 7, 111
Hay MSL 78
Hayes, Robert 31–2
hierarchy
    and deference 64, 85–8
    and delayering 99
Hofstede, Geert 116–17
holidays, amount 109
homogeneity 121
    and systems 80
Hopkins, Harry 17
hospitals
    and competitive advantage 65–6, 67
    and systems 77
hotels, international 30
hours of work 39, 109–10
human nature, perfectibility 68–70, 107
human resource management 3,
        102–14
    and benefits 104–5
    and contract negotiation 46, 83,
        98–101
    and employee morale 105–6
    function 102–3
    and proactivity 103, 104–9
    US and Europe compared 103–9
    see also personnel
humour 88, 110

illiteracy 75–6, 129
imperialism, managerial 125
imports 28
improvement, and proactivity 68–70,
        107–8
individualism 37–48, 60, 79
    and career 40–3
    and communication 81
    and contract negotiation 98
    and economics 128
    in Europe 114
    and generalisation 116–17, 120
    and humour 88
    and mobility 43–6
    and praise 37–9

and recourse to law 108
    and self-depiction 39–40
    and success 46–8, 67
information
    and checking 84–5
    and human resource management
        105, 106
    and knowledge 10–11, 88–9, 110
    and strategy 50, 54, 60
    and systems 16, 79
    use of 11–15, 42
internationalisation
    and managing diversity 130–1
    and strategy 49, 55, 59
investment
    decline 31
    foreign 126
Israel, management 2

Jamieson, Ian 72–3, 74, 76
Japan
    compared with USA 28, 29, 34–5, 100
    and US economic decline 34, 128
job security 111
Joint Productivity Councils 4

knowledge
    and information 10–11, 88–9, 110
    and strategy 52, 55
Kotler, Philip 15

labour
    contracts 45–6, 95, 96, 98–101
    division 67
    poaching 67
    shortage 20, 21, 100
    and systems 76, 79
    turnover 76
    see also personnel
Latin America, growth potential 36
law
    and betterment 68–9, 102, 107–8
    and lawlessness xi, 8, 97–8, 119–20
    recourse to 66–7, 90, 91–2, 108
leadership
    in Europe 113
    in USA 122
Leverhulme, William Hesketh Lever, 1st
        Viscount 15
Levering, Robert 18

Levitt, Theodore 15
lifestyle clusters 13–15, 119

management
 as concept x, 21
 and economic decline 127–8
 homespun style 121–3
 prerogative 4, 8–10, 95, 97, 106, 112
 scientific 3
 self-awareness 2–4, 21
 as subject 3, 18–19, 21
management gap x, 4
manufacturing
 and decline 33–4
 and economic power 20
 and employment 29
 financing 20–1
 location 93–4
 output 23, *24*, *25–7*
marketing
 and information 15
 invention 3, 15, 31
 systems 72–3
materialism, and success xi, 46–8, 49
means and ends
 in Europe 113, 114
 in USA 16–19, 61–2, 81
measurement 74, 110–11
medical services
 and competitive advantage 65–6, 67
 as employee benefit 100, 101, 104–5
 and systems 77
Medicare 77
meetings, and proactivity 64–5
mergers
 and career paths 41, 45
 and strategy 31, 53, 55
migration, industrial 93–4
mission statements 51
MIT, Commission on Industrial
 Productivity 33–4
mobility
 geographic 43, 44, 45, 120, 121
 inter-company 43–6, 52, 120
 intra-company 41–2, 71
 social 44, 45, 120, 121
Moore, J.L. 49
morale, employee 105–6
morality, and proactivity 47–8, 67
Moskowitz, Milton 18

nationality, and individualism
 116–17

opposition, and proactivity 85
optimism, US 16–18
order, as Canadian value 1, 6
organisation, and US superiority 4–5
overtime, in Germany 98

perceptions of USA, and familiarity
 x–xi
perfectibility, belief in 68–70
personnel
 recruitment 74–5
 strategies 57
 and systems 72, 74–5
 training 75–6, 79
 see also human resource management;
  labour
Porras, Jerry 62
Porter, Michael 28, 35
post-industrialism 28
Potter, David 16
power, as resource 85, 88
praise, and individualism 37–9
proactivity 61–70, 79, 111
 and advantage 47, 65–70
 and communication 82
 definition 61
 government 16
 and human resource management
  103, 104–9
 and marketing 73
 and meetings 64–5
 and morality 47–8, 67
 and opposition 85
 and professionalism 124
 and recourse to law 66–7, 91–2
 and subsidiaries 72–3
problem-solving, and proactivity 61, 62,
 64–5
product differentiation 51
productivity levels 31
professionalism, management xi, 4, 80,
 120, 122, 123–5, 127
profits
 and short-termism 127
 and wages 100–1
progress, belief in 68–70
Pyle, Ernie 1

quality, and systems 130
quantification, American penchant for 52, 74, 110–11

railroads, and joint stock finance 20–1
Read, Piers Paul 115–25
receptionists, as non-deferential 86
recruitment, personnel 74–5
regions, and variation 111, 118–21
relations, industrial 18, 93–101
    Britain 9, 99–100
    and industrial democracy 8–10, 97–8
    and strikes 95–7
    Sweden 9, 99
    and system 95
    see also human resource management; labour; trade unionism
remuneration
    and human resource management 8, 106–7
    of management 71
    systems 77–8
    see also benefits; labour, contract
'report-to' 86, 122
resources 16, 20, 23, 26–7
    export 28, 35
retailing
    cross-border 30
    strategies 51–2, 55, 56–7
risk-taking 111
Robbin, Jonathan 13–14, 15
Roosevelt, F. D. 16–17, 110
rules *see* systems

sabotage, and strikes 46, 96
secretaries, as non-deferential 85–6
segmentation, and strategy 30, 54, 55–61
self-consciousness, American 1–4, 5–7, 13
self-depiction 39–40
self-doubt 31–2
self-interest, and speech 90–2
Servan-Schreiber, Jean-Jacques 4–5
service sector 28–32
    and trade balance 29–30
short-termism 31, 122, 127–8
social security, and contract negotiation 99–100, 104

socialism, absence 93
Sombart, Werner 93
specialisation, and strategy 55
speech, quality 90–2
standardisation 30, 79
Stone, Roger 74
strategy 3, 49–60, 79
    and industry developments 55–6
    and information 50, 54, 60
    key decisions 58–60
    Key Success Factors 56–8
    and managers 50–4
    and professionalism 124
    rhetoric and reality 60
    segment-specific 54
    as US invention 49–50
strikes 46, 95–7, 99
style
    homespun 121–3
    professional 120, 122, 123–5
subsidiaries, overseas
    and Americanness x, 3, 32, 71
    and industrial democracy 97–8
    and systems 71, 72–3
success 111, 120
    in Europe 114
    and individualism 46–8, 67
    Key Factors 56–8
    and materialism 48, 49
Sweden
    and individuality 117
    and industrial democracy 9–10
    industrial relations 9, 99
    and internationalisation 130
    and strategy 50
switchboard operators, as non-deferential 86
systems 71–80, 110–11, 123
    and British subsidiaries 71, 72–3
    causes and consequences 78–80
    celebration of 73–4
    and educational standards 129–30
    and efficiency 4, 34, 124
    in Europe 112–13
    and industrial relations 95
    and information 16, 79
    and service sector 30
    and strategy 50
    substance 74–8

targets, and proactivity 61, 62–3
technology
    and competitive advantage 66
    and organisation 4
Texas, management style 119–20
Thurow, Lester 34, 100, 128
total quality management 17
trade, patterns 23–8, 127
trade balance 28, 29–30, 127
trade unionism 10, 34, 45–6
    as avoidable 10, 94–5, 105, 106–7
    and contract negotiation 83, 98–9
    Germany 93, 103
    as non-ideological 93–4, 105
    and strikes 95–7, 99
    Sweden 9
training, systems 75–6, 79

USA
    regional variations 111
    working in 109–14

values, cultural 109–14, 125
Vernon, Raymond 32

Warren, Mike 18
Waterman, Robert 127
wealth 35, 81–2
Weiss, Michael 13–14
women, in management 42–3
work, commitment to 39, 109–10
workers, and management 8–10

zip codes, and lifestyle clusters 13–15,
    119